NUCLEAR ENERGY AND NATIONAL SECURITY

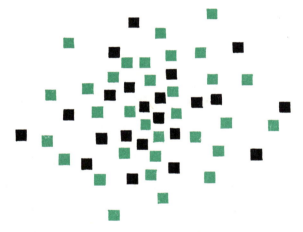

*A Statement on National Policy
by the Research and Policy Committee
of the Committee for Economic Development*

September 1976

Library of Congress Cataloging in Publication Data

Committee for Economic Development.
  Nuclear energy and national security.

    1. Atomic energy industries—United States.
2. Energy policy—United States.   3. United States—
National security.   I. Title.
HD9698.U52C59   1976   333.7   76-28795
ISBN 0-87186-762-1   lib. bdg.
ISBN 0-87186-062-7   pbk.

First printing: September 1976
Paperbound: $2.50
Library binding: $4.00
Printed in the United States of America by Georgian Press, Inc.
Design: Harry Carter

COMMITTEE FOR ECONOMIC DEVELOPMENT
477 Madison Avenue, New York, N.Y. 10022
1700 K Street, N.W., Washington, D.C. 20006

Contents

Responsibility for CED Statements on National Policy

The Committee for Economic Development is an independent research and educational organization of two hundred business executives and educators. CED is nonprofit, nonpartisan, and nonpolitical. Its purpose is to propose policies that will help to bring about steady economic growth at high employment and reasonably stable prices, increase productivity and living standards, provide greater and more equal opportunity for every citizen, and improve the quality of life for all. A more complete description of the objectives and organization of CED is to be found on page 80.

All CED policy recommendations must have the approval of the Research and Policy Committee, a group of sixty trustees whose names are listed on these pages. This Committee is directed under the bylaws to "initiate studies into the principles of business policy and of public policy which will foster the full contribution by industry and commerce to the attainment and maintenance" of the objectives stated above. The bylaws emphasize that "all research is to be thoroughly objective in character, and the approach in each instance is to be from the standpoint of the general welfare and not from that of any special political or economic group." The Committee is aided by a Research Advisory Board of leading social scientists and by a small permanent professional staff.

Research and Policy Committee*

The Research and Policy Committee is not attempting to pass judgment on any pending specific legislative proposals; its purpose is to urge careful consideration of the objectives set forth in this statement and of the best means of accomplishing those objectives.

Each statement on national policy is preceded by discussions, meetings, and exchanges of memoranda, often stretching over many months. The research is undertaken by a subcommittee, assisted by advisors chosen for their competence in the field under study. The members and advisors of the subcommittee that prepared this statement are listed on page 6.

The full Research and Policy Committee participates in the drafting of findings and recommendations. Likewise, the trustees on the drafting subcommittee vote to approve or disapprove a policy statement, and they share with the Research and Policy Committee the privilege of submitting individual comments for publication, as noted on this and the following page and on the appropriate page of the text of the statement.

Except for the members of the Research and Policy Committee and the responsible subcommittee, the recommendations presented herein are not necessarily endorsed by other trustees or by the advisors, contributors, staff members, or others associated with CED.

Subcommittee on Nuclear Energy and National Security

Advisors to the Subcommittee

Project Director

CED Staff Associates

Foreword

Purpose of This Statement

THE USE OF NUCLEAR ENERGY to produce electric power is a fact of life, both in the United States and around the world. Over thirty countries already have, or have begun work on, nuclear power reactors, and even more have some other type of nuclear capability. Although there has been much debate concerning this country's own nuclear future, it is also a fact of life that regardless of what the United States does, the worldwide use of nuclear power will continue to grow until it can be replaced economically by power derived directly from the sun's radiation.

Most of the attention in this country has been focused on the expansion of domestic nuclear power. However, the gravest threat to U.S. security comes from the fact that more national nuclear power programs around the world mean proliferation of materials that could be used in nuclear weapons. If the reprocessing of spent reactor fuel to retrieve plutonium and the use of that plutonium in breeder reactors become common, the resulting plutonium economy would make weapons-grade material available to dozens of countries.

A DILEMMA FOR THE UNITED STATES

There is no way for the United States to isolate itself from these developments, and government policy must recognize that nuclear energy is an issue in which domestic and international interests are inseparable. The United States no longer has anything approaching a monopoly on nuclear technology. It can no longer stop the growth of nuclear power (if indeed it ever could). The United States might conceivably reduce its own energy consumption sufficiently to be able to rely primarily on coal when supplies of oil and gas give out, but many other nations do not have that option. However, this country is still in an influential position, and if it wishes to have any say at all in the safe and controlled development of nuclear power, it simply cannot afford to withdraw from the nuclear world.

The purpose of this statement is to explore ways to prevent or at least to slow the spread of individual national capabilities to produce nuclear explosives while still meeting the world's needs for energy. The spread of nuclear technology may be inevitable, but a multitude of national facilities for enriching uranium or extracting plutonium is not. There is still time, we believe, for the United States and other concerned countries to restrain and safeguard the nuclear power industry through export controls, improved inspection, and multinational control of dangerous nuclear materials.

The problems are serious, but we believe something can be done. Like the rest of the world, the United States will have to get used to living with new and inescapable dangers. Although civilian nuclear power reactors raise serious health and environmental questions, the truly horrendous dangers we face will develop beyond U.S. control. By the year 2000, the total plutonium produced as a by-product of global nuclear power will be the equivalent of 1 million atomic bombs. The worst hazards will come, not from U.S. enrichment of uranium or separation of plutonium for its own power plants, but from up to 100 countries that may be doing the same thing.

Until recently, a country that wanted nuclear weapons had to build them directly. Now, with the raw materials for such weapons becoming increasingly available, many countries will find the decision threshold significantly lowered. Without strong international commitment to nonproliferation agreements, it could become almost irresistibly easy for a nonnuclear power to turn the corner and acquire its own nuclear arsenal.

Our report does not offer recommendations that can solve this very difficult problem. In fact, there may be no real solutions. But it does offer some first steps toward dealing with the political and technical problems and toward lessening the risks of rapid nuclear expansion.

The subcommittee that prepared this report examined the question with great thoroughness and care and came to the conclusion that the

United States really has no choice. Its only option is to continue to participate in the nuclear world, to exercise as much influence and leadership as it can to see that the worst catastrophes of such a world do not come to pass.

WHAT CAN BE DONE

The United States must first recognize that it does not have a domestic energy problem and a separate international energy problem. They are one problem. Foreign and domestic energy decisions can no longer be treated separately; they must be part of a clear, unified national security policy involving both Congress and the highest levels of the executive branch.

Armed with an effective energy policy, the United States can be in a strong position to negotiate for increased international safeguards. It can help strengthen the International Atomic Energy Agency's inspection capability and can negotiate with all nuclear-trading countries to attach common safeguards to all sales and to the handling of nuclear materials and wastes.

Crucial decisions will hinge on how scarce or plentiful uranium ore is in the United States and around the world. We believe that the United States must vigorously pursue its exploration for uranium ore in this country and develop cooperative methods for estimating supplies in other parts of the world. If countries that do not have the capacity to enrich uranium for reactor fuel can be assured a continuous supply at reasonable prices, the incentive to build their own enrichment plants may be reduced.

DEVELOPING SUPPLY

If reserves of high-grade uranium are found insufficient for future needs and the use of plutonium as a reactor fuel becomes economic, the problem of controlling access to dangerous materials becomes even more critical. We believe that placing facilities for uranium enrichment and plutonium extraction under the control of several nations might prevent such facilities from being developed independently by individual nations. We further suggest that if the United States wishes to encourage such multilateral arrangements, it should consider making some of its own facilities available through such an international program.

The enormous and complex problems of global nuclear power demand that private enterprise work in close cooperation with government. There is, we feel, an essential diplomatic role for the federal government and an equally essential productive and commercial role for private enterprise. In certain areas requiring exceptionally large capital investment, such as the expansion of uranium-enrichment capacity, the federal government should assume comprehensive financial risk.

This statement has its roots in CED's previous work in national security and energy policy. In 1972, we issued our first statement in these areas: *Military Manpower and National Security*. In 1974, we issued *Congressional Decision Making for National Security*, which proposed measures to equip Congress to perform its role in the national security area. CED's first statement on energy policy, *Achieving Energy Independence*, also published in 1974, proposed measures to stimulate domestic energy production and reduce the growth of demand to bring about U.S. energy independence by 1985. *International Economic Consequences of High-Priced Energy* (1975) presented an assessment of worldwide energy-based economic problems by CED and six international counterparts.

The present report follows and builds on our previous studies by tying together domestic and international energy problems and world security problems related to the spread of nuclear weapons.

ACKNOWLEDGMENTS

The subcommittee that prepared this report included trustees and advisors with impressive backgrounds in business, government, and technology. A list of its members appears on page 6. The Research and Policy Committee extends special thanks to project director Thomas C. Schelling of the John F. Kennedy School of Government at Harvard University for his clear and incisive approach to this problem that will affect all our lives.

Philip M. Klutznick, *Chairman*
Research and Policy Committee
until May 19, 1976

Franklin A. Lindsay, *Chairman*
Research and Policy Committee
beginning May 20, 1976

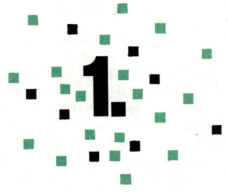

Introduction
and Summary
of Recommendations

As AMERICANS WEIGH THE ISSUES of living with nuclear energy, one important fact is often overlooked: Nuclear energy is a reality in the rest of the world. About 30 countries have already begun installing nuclear reactors. In twenty years, 100 countries will possess the raw materials and the knowledge necessary to produce nuclear bombs. There is no way that the United States can remain isolated from global developments of such magnitude. The nation must decide what its role will be in the coming world nuclear economy. Nuclear energy and its consequences for national security are life-and-death matters deserving the highest priority on the national agenda.*

It is fallacious to believe that this country can escape the hazards of worldwide nuclear development by forgoing its economic advantages at home. It is equally fallacious to believe that the United States need be concerned only with domestic costs and benefits, as if the perils of nuclear development in the rest of the world could be safely ignored. U.S. policy must recognize that nuclear energy is an issue in which it is impossible to separate U.S. and world interests. Nuclear power has the most wide-ranging implications not only for worldwide energy needs but also for the domestic and international economies and for national defense and indeed the security of all nations. *Acute national security interests and urgent economic and environmental interests at home are inextricably inter-*

*See memoranda by CHARLES P. BOWEN, Jr., by LINCOLN GORDON, and by PHILIP SPORN, pages 66 and 67.

twined. They cannot be separated from similar interests of other countries. Failure of the U.S. government to recognize these interrelated issues and to deal with them in a coherent and comprehensive manner could be disastrous.

This policy statement is intended to increase awareness of these nuclear issues. The recommendations that we offer are not solutions to the problems raised by worldwide nuclear development, but they do describe positive steps that the United States can take toward finding solutions. Although the problems are enormous and disheartening, ignorance of nuclear choices and perils can only make the world more dangerous than it already threatens to be. Nuclear energy almost certainly will be essential to meeting the world's future energy needs, but its weapon potential is a threat to the very existence of all nations.

NUCLEAR ENERGY AND ITS ALTERNATIVES

This Committee examined the various alternative sources of energy in the policy statement *Achieving Energy Independence* (1974). We stated there our belief that nuclear power, subject to adequate safeguards including waste disposal, promises to be the solution to many of the difficulties associated with fossil fuels. We reaffirm that view. For the United States, the difficulties associated with fossil fuels are environmental, economic, and strategic. For other countries, the difficulties connected with dependence upon oil and coal are even more acute. Consequently, nuclear power will provide a substantial portion of the world's expanding energy needs between now and the year 2000.

At the same time, the United States is one of the few countries that may have any real choice between nuclear power and an alternative that has a proven supply and an available technology. That alternative is coal. The use of coal will almost certainly have to double within the next decade and will have to increase still further by the end of the century. The growth of electric power during the next several decades will be significant, and a shift to uranium and coal as fuels for the generation of electricity will be essential.

Other new sources of energy should be vigorously explored. Unfortunately, the pursuit of alternatives has intensified the debate between proponents of nuclear energy and proponents of nonnuclear alternatives. Advocates of nuclear energy often disparage other sources of energy; advocates of nonnuclear sources tend to offer alternatives (such as solar

Figure 1: U.S. ENERGY CONSUMPTION, 1900–1975 *(quadrillion BTUs)*

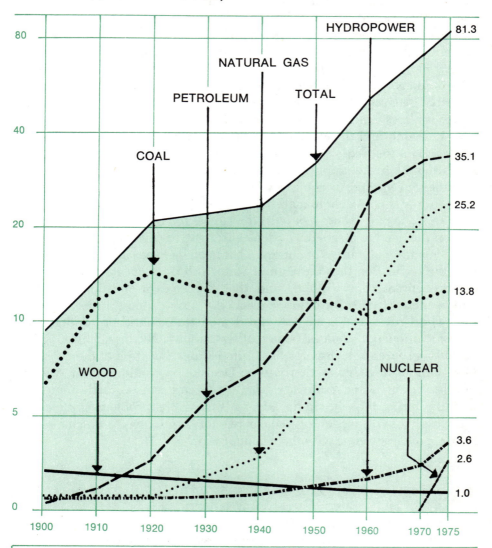

SOURCES: Data for 1900 to 1970: U.S. Bureau of the Census, *Historical Abstracts of the United States* (Washington, D.C.: U.S. Government Printing Office, 1975). Data for 1975: U.S. Bureau of the Census, *Statistical Abstracts of the United States* (Washington, D.C.: U.S. Government Printing Office, 1975).

energy), not as complements to, but as substitutes for, nuclear power. We deplore this tendency to treat complementary sources of energy as though they were mutually exclusive. Nuclear, solar, and geothermal energy; coal and synthetics derived from coal; and major energy conservation measures are not conflicting alternatives. On the contrary, combining development and conservation of energy resources is the first step to achieving energy independence. That is emphatically true for Japan and for many other nations whose dependence on foreign oil can seriously weaken U.S. security. Because of uncertainty and delay in the development of new energy sources, conservation becomes all the more important.

Research and development of solar energy should be pressed seriously and undoubtedly will proceed both in the United States and abroad. But although a few applications are approaching cost effectiveness, the technology required to achieve substantial economy through the use of solar energy is not likely to materialize in the immediate future.

In *Achieving Energy Independence,* we focused considerable attention on the need to assess the outlook and relative efficiencies of both new and conventional sources of energy. That need becomes more urgent as we face the realization that the United States still does not have a clear and comprehensive energy policy and that the goal of substantial energy independence by 1985 will not be reached.

The United States has also not demonstrated sufficient understanding of the energy choices facing other nations. Nuclear power is one promising source of energy for the United States, but it is not the only one. Most nations have fewer alternatives. Decisions to build nuclear reactors in other countries have already been made and will be made more frequently during the coming decade.* Although the problems entailed by the worldwide dispersion of nuclear reactors are largely problems of the future, policies to cope with them cannot wait.

NUCLEAR PROLIFERATION
AND A PLUTONIUM ECONOMY

Until recently, *nuclear proliferation* referred to actual possession of weapons or to a demonstrated possession of nuclear explosives motivated by an express decision for a nuclear capability. But the meaning of the term *nuclear proliferation* is undergoing a dramatic change. In another ten or fifteen years, most nations will have the technical ability to produce nuclear explosives from reactor fuel. The basic material needed to make a

*See memorandum by PHILIP SPORN, page 68.

plutonium bomb, the plutonium itself, is generated in a nuclear reactor as a by-product of producing steam for the generation of electricity. It can be separated from the rest of the spent fuel and refined into a form suitable for use in a weapon. This can be done quite openly under the Treaty on the Non-Proliferation of Nuclear Weapons as long as the International Atomic Energy Agency (IAEA) can monitor and inspect the process in accordance with the treaty's safeguards provision. Thus, whether or not they possess actual stockpiles of weapons, most nations will possess the materials base and the technological base for producing nuclear weapons. In that sense—and it is a terribly dangerous sense—worldwide nuclear proliferation will occur in the early, if not the immediate, future.

Commercial-scale reprocessing of plutonium is not yet being done. In the United States, the regulations under which a reprocessing plant might operate and plutonium might be handled have not been decided and, according to the Nuclear Regulatory Commission (NRC), are not expected to be until next year.[1] Aside from legal sanctions, cost is the practical barrier to using recycled plutonium and uranium to provide some 10 or 20 percent of the total required fuel. At present, it is not clear whether these materials can be extracted and used as fuel for less than the cost of an equivalent amount of new uranium. Therefore, most countries that burn nuclear fuel in power reactors will for a time continue to depend on imported uranium fuel of a kind that is useless for weapons. But it must be remembered that when such uranium fuel is consumed in a reactor, the plutonium that results (if it is successfully separated from the rods of spent reactor fuel) suffers no such disability. It can indeed be used to make bombs. Therefore, even before plutonium recycling becomes economic, the creation of plutonium will pose a severe threat to national security.

A key factor in the economic feasibility of plutonium reprocessing is the cost of uranium. The future price of uranium is uncertain. It may double or quadruple by the 1990s as the supply of high-grade ore becomes exhausted, and unless some unexpected technologies for extracting uranium economically from seawater or from low-grade ores are discovered—and in an environmentally acceptable manner—it may be only a matter of time before it becomes economic to extract plutonium from spent fuel and

---

[1] In January 1975, the Atomic Energy Commission was superseded by the Energy Research and Development Agency and the Nuclear Regulatory Commission. NRC exercises the licensing and other regulatory functions concerned with nuclear safety and security.

to recycle it into a reactor. If, instead, the price of uranium goes down, it may not pay to reprocess fuel.

A decision to proceed with commercial reprocessing of plutonium would encourage the development of the *breeder reactor* (a reactor that produces more plutonium than it consumes). If breeder reactors can be developed as an economic and reliable source of power, they will have two enormously important effects. They will postpone for more than 100 years the prospect of a shortage of fuel for nuclear reactors. And they will ensure the emergence of the *plutonium economy*, with all its dangers.

If the plutonium economy becomes a reality, a country interested in acquiring at least a limited nuclear weapons capability could easily disguise that interest by stressing the economic case for investing in nuclear reactors to meet its energy needs. Inventories of plutonium or plutonium fuel assemblies would be common. World trade in plutonium or plutonium fuel assemblies would be common. Like gold, plutonium will have to be carefully guarded in storage and shipment. Unlike gold, an amount of plutonium that a person can carry in one hand can be made into a bomb powerful enough to destroy a city.

The Non-Proliferation Treaty forbids signatories, except those already identified as nuclear weapons states (states that had exploded a nuclear device before January 1, 1967), from using their plutonium to make bombs.[2] It obliges nonnuclear weapons states to submit their reactors, their spent-fuel depots, any chemical-processing facilities, any plutonium inventories, and any fuel fabricated out of plutonium to scrutiny by IAEA inspectors.

Yet, with a decade of lead time in which to plan, it seems likely that governments anticipating the possession of a physical capability to fabricate nuclear weapons will take steps to develop personnel or laboratory teams acquainted with the technology and perhaps practiced in the pertinent operations. It is generally acknowledged that most of the scientific and technical information needed to make a bomb out of plutonium or highly enriched uranium is publicly available and not difficult to obtain. Furthermore, the motive and the ability to keep weapons designs secret

---

[2]The Treaty on the Non-Proliferation of Nuclear Weapons was signed July 1, 1968, by the governments of the United States, the United Kingdom, and the Soviet Union and went into force March 5, 1970, upon ratification by forty other governments. Ninety-eight nations are parties to the treaty, and another thirteen have signed but have not completed ratification.

will diminish as more countries investigate the subject and as it is increasingly taken for granted that the knowledge is becoming widely available.

In a military sense, therefore, scores of countries, perhaps most countries, will have nuclear weapons. That is, they will have access to them. Upon any decision to proceed with assembly, test, demonstration, or military use, a growing inventory could be available on a predictable schedule with a brief lag of weeks or days rather than months. If independent national chemical-reprocessing facilities for the separation of plutonium or facilities for the enrichment of uranium become generally available, the countries possessing them will possess nuclear mobilization bases that could be activated in any emergency in which a country was willing to withdraw from or violate any nonproliferation commitment it had undertaken.[3]

The dangers in such a world are not limited to those that may be caused by the belligerency or irresponsibility of national governments. Fissionable materials in various forms will be stored in many locations and will be shipped by various modes of transport from fuel-fabrication facilities to power stations; spent fuel will be shipped from reactors to reprocessing facilities; plutonium will be shipped from reprocessing facilities to storage sites or fuel-assembly facilities. It will be an endless cycle. The number of shipments of potentially explosive materials within or between countries may be tens of thousands per year. As is the case with any valuable or dangerous material, there will be the possibility of theft or hijacking for criminal or terrorist purposes or for other illicit use by individuals, organizations, or movements. It is worth pondering that even several NATO countries have been subject to military revolt, usually with the military forces divided politically.

POLICY DILEMMA

The world's use of energy in all its forms has more than doubled every fifteen years since 1925. For several decades, the major source has been petroleum. To a substantial extent, the demand for continued economic development in both the industrialized and the undeveloped coun-

---

[3]On three months' notice, a party to the Non-Proliferation Treaty can withdraw if "extraordinary events, related to the subject matter of this treaty, have jeopardized the supreme interests of its country."

PLUTONIUM'S EXPLOSIVE POTENTIAL

The enormous energy embodied in uranium fuels for reactors is not an immediate military threat; these fuels will be imported, inventoried, and slowly consumed. Nevertheless, the plutonium produced within the power reactor, as a by-product, is potentially explosive. And as explosives, the amounts are staggering.

Here are the customary estimates: Two decades from now, the plutonium produced in electric power reactors outside the United States and the Soviet Union would, if chemically processed, be sufficient to produce more than 10,000 atomic bombs per year. By the year 2000, the total plutonium expected to have been produced as a by-product of nuclear power would be equivalent in explosive potential to 1 million bombs of the size that destroyed Nagasaki.

A conservative estimate would be as follows: Worldwide electrical capacity will have quadrupled by the year 2000. If the increase were one-third nuclear, there would be well over 1 billion kilowatts of nuclear generating capacity; this would produce about 250,000 kilograms of plutonium in a year, potentially equivalent to tens of thousands of atomic bombs. (See the discussion of critical mass as a unit of measure, page 32.)

tries of the world will be a demand for a continued increase in the use of energy, especially electricity. Thus, by strategic choice or by necessity, most countries are going to make increasing use of nuclear energy.

The drastically changed nature of the proliferation problem, from a weapons orientation to an energy orientation with weapons implications, poses a dilemma for the security of the United States that will require wisdom and subtlety in the formulation of U.S. policy. *It is no longer within the power of the United States, if indeed it ever was, to prevent the rest of the world from moving toward nuclear electric power.* Furthermore, the United States is committed by the Non-Proliferation Treaty (in the negotiation of which the United States took a leading role) to facili-

Figure 2: WORLD ENERGY CONSUMPTION TRENDS, 1960–1990 *(quadrillion BTUs)*

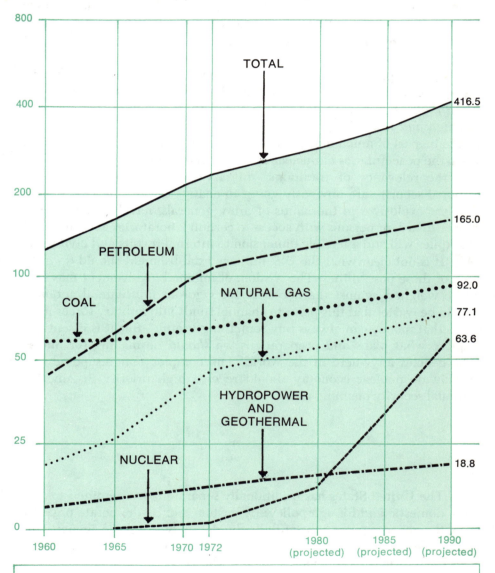

SOURCE: U.S. Department of the Interior, *Energy Perspectives* (Washington, D.C.: U.S. Government Printing Office, February 1975).

tate "the fullest possible exchange of equipment, materials and scientific and technological information for the peaceful uses of nuclear energy." The diplomatic basis for safeguarding nuclear materials and facilities will rest on the confidence that governments have in that treaty and on the good faith they display and expect from each other in conforming to its spirit and letter.

For the past decade, U.S. efforts to cope with nuclear proliferation have been focused on the Non-Proliferation Treaty. *But it must be recognized that a significant fraction of the world's governments will probably not sign and ratify the Non-Proliferation Treaty.* Henceforth, the treaty has to be part of much more complicated legal and diplomatic safeguards upon the peaceful uses of nuclear energy.* The nature of national security and the relevance of traditional military forces and expenditures to national security are obviously going to change during the next decade. Nuclear explosives in the hands of army generals, naval commanders, a palace guard, or persons with access to certain laboratories and plutonium stockpiles will add a terrible dimension to internal revolts and civil wars.

It is not clear what the U.S. military establishment should do in the face of these possibilities. The wisdom of minimal involvement may have to be weighed against the necessity for vigorous multilateral action. It would be wasteful at this point to channel funds into military forces in the hope that money can always buy something useful.* But it is essential to explore what plans and preparations we *should* be making for nuclear emergencies anywhere in the world. The complex dangers posed by a worldwide nuclear economy should receive high priority in American national security planning now.

ORGANIZING GOVERNMENT FOR A COHERENT POLICY

The United States has traditionally separated, or attempted to separate, domestic and foreign policy. By custom and by deliberate organization, the government is substantially divided between those agencies that have little or no responsibility for what goes on abroad and those agencies that have little or no responsibility for what goes on at home.

The single pervasive issue of nuclear energy demands a coherent set of policies reflecting the energy interdependence of the U.S. economy and the rest of the world. These policies will require painful readjustments in the way the U.S. government makes policies and programs and

*See memoranda by PHILIP SPORN, pages 68 and 69.

carries them out. The U.S. government must quickly develop a new capability to deal coherently with matters that are of the most urgent economic significance domestically and of the highest diplomatic and security significance abroad.

At present, there are a number of political initiatives to fragment energy policy by making it the responsibility of the fifty individual states. If the object of these initiatives is obstruction, they represent a particularly futile and localized isolationism. If their object is assuring that energy policy is responsible to the local and regional needs of people, we believe that they are misguided. In the development of new sources of energy, in the provision of incentives to conserve energy, in the balancing of energy needs against the social costs of exploiting resources, and especially in the recognition of the problems of worldwide nuclear energy, this nation cannot afford to have fifty separate energy policies. Security against the hazards of nuclear energy requires that the problems be faced on a scale larger than that of a single country, not fifty times smaller. Indeed, a unified national policy will be inadequate unless it is coordinated at the very least with the countries participating in the International Energy Agency (IEA).

The United States cannot have a nuclear energy foreign policy unless it has an energy policy. It cannot have a foreign policy on reactor fuel supplies if it has no policy for domestic production of fuel. It cannot have a foreign policy on reprocessing of spent fuel without settling domestic policy. The United States cannot take the lead in solving worldwide problems of spent-fuel storage and waste disposal if it has no adequate plan for domestic storage and disposal or for participation in a larger plan. In general, this nation cannot assume any leadership or use whatever influence it might have in shaping the worldwide development of nuclear power except in coordination with domestic nuclear policies.

Sensible energy planning in the United States must start by replacing the divisive ideological controversies about nuclear power with some basic understandings. This country needs a wider agreement that nuclear power does indeed raise severe problems, including hazards that are poorly understood and that may occur on an unprecedented scale. However severe these problems are, they have to be acknowledged in order to be solved. It is important to recognize that not all the problems can be solved to everybody's satisfaction in a hurry. And it is necessary to recognize that high employment and a better standard of living will require meeting increasing demands for energy.*

The development and conservation of energy resources will be

*See memorandum by LINCOLN GORDON, page 69.

central to the development of the U.S. economy during the coming decades. The increasing importance of energy policy was recognized by this Committee in *Achieving Energy Independence,* in which we recommended that energy policy be the responsibility of a new cabinet-level agency. We reassert that recommendation. **We urge that any organizational arrangements for energy policy be undertaken with full recognition of the inseparability of the foreign and domestic aspects of national strategy for energy. From now on, energy policy must be considered an integral part of national security policy, and the highest level of presidential authority must be responsible for it.** U.S. energy policy will be highly influential in U.S. efforts to safeguard the worldwide nuclear economy and will be at the center of this nation's strategic relations with many important countries.

The Senate and the House of Representatives are not organized for effectively dealing with the complex field of energy policy, especially for integrating long-term energy policy with foreign policy and national security. Like the executive branch, Congress has traditionally been accustomed to dealing with foreign problems and domestic problems separately. **We recommend that Congress take steps similar to those recommended by this Committee in 1974 for the executive branch to recognize that energy policy is simultaneously central to the domestic economy and to national security.**

NEGOTIATING INTERNATIONAL SAFEGUARDS

The U.S. government must simultaneously honor its commitments to certain kinds of nuclear favoritism and maintain the flexibility necessary for further diplomatic progress in nuclear matters. What will make this policy a demanding one is that it has to be reflected not only at the high level of explicit diplomacy but also in all the programs and operations dealing with the licensing and financing of nuclear exports, commitments for the delivery of nuclear fuel, technical cooperation and assistance, and alliance relationships.

We strongly recommend that the United States negotiate with all nuclear-supplying countries, including those that are not signatories of the Treaty on the Non-Proliferation of Nuclear Weapons, to attach common International Atomic Energy Agency safeguards on all sales to all countries. Such safeguards should be more stringent than they are now and should apply not only to the actual facilities and materials exported

but also to any indigenous production of nuclear facilities or materials.

IAEA safeguards are an important step toward controlling nuclear dangers, but their effectiveness should not be overstated. Even the term *safeguards* is misleading. Current IAEA safeguards amount only to inspection, surveillance, and record keeping; they are not *physical* safeguards.

If a country does violate safeguard agreements, IAEA can only sound an alarm. There is no mechanism for dealing with a country or individual that has broken a safeguard agreement, nor has any party to the Non-Proliferation Treaty proposed such a mechanism. IAEA can only alert the United States and other countries to problems; in the end, these problems must be dealt with by political means.

Successful negotiation of safeguards and restrictions will require effective federal control over the export of nuclear equipment, materials, and technology and vigorous efforts to work out common terms and conditions of nuclear exports with the governments of other nuclear-exporting countries. Relaxation of safeguards must not be allowed to become a method of competition in the nuclear-export market.

It is time to begin planning with other countries for coping with nuclear emergencies. Governments could decide to abrogate the safeguards they had accepted under the Non-Proliferation Treaty or under other arrangements and proceed to build nuclear explosives. Nuclear accidents can occur. Sabotage or occupation of nuclear facilities may be attempted. Nonnational organizations or dissident military forces may acquire nuclear materials. Internal security threats will have terrifying implications for other countries when they become nuclear threats.

The United States needs to develop new methods of technical surveillance and intelligence, mostly in cooperation with other governments, to cope with this range of security and safety problems. **The United States should support efforts to enlarge very substantially the inspection capability of the International Atomic Energy Agency, both through increased personnel and through the development and installation of the most modern techniques of automatic surveillance and materials control.**

Another problem U.S. nuclear energy foreign policy must address is the disposal of nuclear wastes and the handling of other environmental hazards. Waste disposal should be closely linked to safeguarding fuel supplies because the shipment of spent fuel to international storage facilities or to storage facilities within the fuel-producing countries would determine the location of those raw materials from which plutonium could be extracted. **We recommend that the United States participate in the** collaborative development of techniques and facilities for handling international shipments of nuclear materials and for disposing of radioactive waste materials in order to achieve common standards of physical security and safety.

IAEA is examining a proposal for internationally owned and managed nuclear fuel centers. The significance of the proposal would be economic and strategic: Many countries that might otherwise proceed to develop independent capabilities for reprocessing plutonium or for enriching uranium fuel might be attracted to the greater economies of larger-scale centralized facilities and also to the greater protection offered by a scheme that would commit other countries to return spent fuel to an internationally managed central location for storage or reprocessing. Although this proposal does not answer the crucial question of what is to be done with these dangerous materials, the United States has expressed interest in it as one further way to reduce the incentives for additional countries to develop their own fuel facilities, which might be usable for the production of weapons material. The United States should be prepared to consider contributing to the success of multilateral arrangements, possibly by making its own enrichment facilities available to participants in such an international program.*

To reduce the incentives for developing indigenous uranium-enrichment or plutonium-reprocessing facilities that might be usable for the production of weapons material, the United States should be prepared to offer, and to collaborate with other countries in offering, assured supplies of reactor fuel on long-term contracts at reasonable prices.** Many of the dangers of the plutonium economy and of the proliferation of uranium enrichment are going to be dangers to which all the countries participating in these nuclear developments will be susceptible. These are dangers to which their governments should become increasingly sensitive as the nature of a possible proliferated world becomes more widely understood. Skillful diplomacy may harness the self-interest of many countries.

GOVERNMENT AND INDUSTRY

An unresolved issue of nuclear energy policy is the proper role of the U.S. government in the ownership or control of production facilities for nuclear fuel. All uranium enrichment in the United States is now done by the federal government, using facilities originally built for weapons programs. Further development of uranium enrichment will be

*See memorandum by LINCOLN GORDON, page 69.
**See memorandum by CHARLES P. BOWEN, Jr., page 69.

for power reactors; therefore, from now on, the major use of the enrichment facilities originally designed for the production of weapons-grade uranium will be production of reactor fuel.

The key point for the United States is that there is an essential diplomatic role for the federal government parallel to an essential production and commercial role for private enterprise. Coordinating these two roles is an immediate challenge.

It has become clear that an early expansion of uranium enrichment will depend on the traditional technology of gaseous diffusion and that private companies will not finance this development without comprehensive federal guarantees of a kind that may not be forthcoming. What makes the matter serious is that the supply of nuclear reactor fuel is one of the few potential inducements that the U.S. government may have at its disposal during the coming decade in helping to shape the development of the worldwide nuclear fuel cycle. We believe that private industry in cooperation with government should competitively develop the forthcoming centrifuge process of uranium enrichment. **But it is urgent to proceed with the next stage of expansion using the older technology. We expect government assumption of financial risks to be comprehensive whether this interim stage is conducted publicly or privately.***

NRC has the power to license, or withhold licensing from, the reprocessing of spent fuel. It is within the authority of NRC to determine whether the process is too hazardous. Like other pending decisions about nuclear energy, this one is charged with foreign policy implications. *A "go" decision by NRC would be a strong signal to the rest of the world that plutonium recycling is a part of the nuclear future. A negative decision by NRC would slow and discourage the development of the plutonium economy.** What needs emphasis is that a decision on reprocessing spent fuel and extracting plutonium is a decision of enormous consequence both for the domestic economy and society and for U.S. foreign policy and national security. The U.S. government must integrate national and international economic and security implications in decisions of this sort.

U.S. ROLE IN GLOBAL NUCLEAR DEVELOPMENT

Whatever happens, there will be no easy solutions to the security problems associated with the worldwide development of nuclear energy. But without vigorous U.S. participation in that development, there may

*See memoranda by LINCOLN GORDON, page 70.

be no solutions at all. It is simply not within the power of the United States to determine unilaterally how nuclear energy is going to develop around the world. The only way in which this country can have a voice in the responsible and orderly development and safe management of this very dangerous technology is by participating in some cooperative arrangements. *We believe there is no choice. Only by continuing to exercise leadership in the worldwide development of atomic energy can the United States hope to influence the way the world's nuclear economy is safeguarded.* Withdrawal of U.S. support from peaceful nuclear developments abroad or renouncing nuclear energy in this country and suppressing its technological development would nullify whatever moderating influence the United States can hope to exercise through continued leadership and cooperation.

The U.S. government is still in a position to influence the worldwide development of nuclear energy—but diplomatically, not unilaterally. It has bargaining power, not decisive leverage. The United States is rapidly losing its preeminence in the field of nuclear technology, reactor exports, and fuel supply. U.S. supply of nuclear fuel, though momentarily adequate, has been committed far in advance. This country's hobbled position as a supplier means that it is unable to offer a crucial inducement to other countries to abstain from developing fuel facilities with weapons potential. Countries dependent on imports of nuclear fuel will need to be assured that there is an adequate supply for their current reactor operations and even for stockpiling abroad.*

In short, a vigorous policy might yet enable the United States to lead and shape world development, use, and control of nuclear energy. Even so, nuclear diplomacy is likely to be frustrating, unsatisfying, and only partially successful. But the frustrations cannot be avoided by abandoning the effort and concentrating on domestic energy development. The United States cannot bury its head in the sand and leave the rest of its body unprotected.

Under these circumstances, it is important to remember that the United States happens to possess some two-fifths of the known high-grade uranium ore in the world (excluding the Soviet Union and the People's Republic of China). There are large uncertainties in estimates of uranium reserves; the extent of undiscovered uranium deposits is not known. The United States is in a strong *potential* position to supply itself, to supply others, and to participate in worldwide arrangements for the harnessing of this enormously important energy resource and thus to establish a strong bargaining position in determining the course that the

*See memorandum by JAMES T. HILL, Jr., page 70.

development of the world nuclear power industry should take. But this potential can be dissipated if the United States fails to take steps to consolidate its position.

Crucial decisions will hinge on just how scarce or plentiful uranium ore is in the United States and around the world and on just how great the costs of extraction will be. Improved estimates through exploration must be considered urgent. Many issues of national policy, both foreign and domestic, will hinge on the knowledge that can be gained.

We recommend that the United States vigorously pursue its program of exploration of uranium deposits within this country and develop cooperative methods for estimating supplies of uranium ore in other parts of the world. Such a course will make it easier to estimate the availability of this important but limited resource to meet U.S. needs and the needs of other countries and to estimate the future demand for new technologies, such as breeder reactors or plutonium recycling, in an open, multinational process that takes adequate account of the needs of other countries. **In addition, we urge that all present restrictions on the importation of foreign uranium be immediately removed.**

Even if nuclear fuel had no explosive potential, managing the world's energy resources would be one of the most challenging elements of American foreign policy. But because the world's next fuel for electricity is also the fuel for the world's most terrifying weapons, hardly anything will determine the physical security of American citizens in future decades more than the way this country utilizes its economic, military, and diplomatic influence in shaping the worldwide development of nuclear energy.

Wars and military emergencies are conditions under which governments that *have* nuclear weapons might consider *using* nuclear weapons. In twenty years, most of the world's governments will *have* (and will be *known* to have) a capacity to mobilize nuclear materials and nuclear technology into nuclear weapons. The most fundamental problem of international security will then be to prevent any interest in using nuclear weapons from ever being realized.*

*See memorandum by PHILIP SPORN, page 70.

Nuclear Energy
and National Security:
Facing the Connection

THE DEBATE OVER NUCLEAR ENERGY has produced several legal and political efforts to prevent the further development of nuclear power within U.S. borders. Opponents of nuclear power rightly point to some of the unprecedented dangers of nuclear accidents and terrorism that may result from the widespread use of nuclear fuel, shipments of nuclear fuel, and storage or treatment of burnt fuel. But their warning fails to recognize that the worst of those dangers will have to be faced and dealt with whether or not the United States utilizes nuclear energy.

Throughout the world, the production of electric power is going to be much less dependent on petroleum and much more dependent on other energy sources during the coming decades. By choice or by necessity, most countries, whether developed or undeveloped, are going to use nuclear energy for electric power. Almost certainly, the same source of energy that is present in the most awesome weapons is going to be used on a massive scale for the production of electricity. There is no way that this source of energy can be tamed, denatured, or otherwise denied its potential for being a ubiquitous source of the raw materials for atomic bombs.

Most countries could develop a nuclear mobilization base as a by-product of the development of electric power and the probable associated development of a plutonium economy. They could develop a capability to proceed promptly with the assembly of nuclear weapons in any emergency in which they were willing to withdraw from or violate the Non-Proliferation Treaty or any other treaties, agreements, or contractual arrangements to which they were party.

The crucial technical fact is that the spent fuel from nuclear power reactors is a basic raw material from which plutonium can be chemically separated. Plutonium is one of the materials from which atomic bombs can be made. Separating the plutonium from the remainder of the spent fuel is not an easy task, but it is within the engineering capabilities of forty or fifty countries, and it is probably no more difficult or demanding than many of the tasks that competent engineering firms from the industrially developed countries contract to perform in even the least developed countries.

We are entering an era in which the raw materials for nuclear explosives are almost certain to multiply and be produced in virtually every country of the world. Less certain, but nevertheless likely, are both the area of the technology and the facilities for extracting plutonium from the spent nuclear fuels and also the burgeoning of technology and facilities to enrich uranium in the isotope uranium 235 for use as a nuclear fuel. Such facilities could be used to enrich the uranium sufficiently to make it as useful as plutonium in the fabrication of nuclear weapons. Many (if not most) countries may then come to possess the stuff of which nuclear explosives are made and the technology by which such weapons can be made.

TIMETABLE

Nuclear Energy Resources. It is uncertain when the known world supply of uranium available at prices comparable to those recently prevailing will be exhausted. But it is likely to be exhausted within the useful lifetime of power reactors being constructed during the next five or ten years. The anticipation of as much as a quadrupling of the price of uranium fuel will affect any government or private plans for the installation of nuclear power during the coming decade.

There is great uncertainty about the amounts of uranium ore that could be available at prices up to five times the present price. Such an increase would amount to about a doubling of the price of reactor fuel and a 15 to 20 percent increase in the cost of electricity. Any nation that invests heavily in nuclear power reactors during the coming decade will be motivated to economize nuclear fuels and to consider the likelihood that facilities for plutonium separation, even if not now economic, may become so within the period of a nuclear power development plan.[1]

The question of how much enrichment capacity will eventually be needed depends on the growth rate of the nuclear industry. There is now, and will be for at least the next few years, an excess of enrichment capacity because the peak demand for enriched uranium under the Energy Research and Development Agency's existing contracts will not occur until the mid-1980s.

Plutonium Reprocessing. The possible economies of recycling plutonium from the present generation of reactors are very small in terms of the overall cost of nuclear electricity, perhaps 1 or 2 percent. The future role of plutonium is not yet clear. Reactors now being built use uranium as fuel. The nuclear fission that occurs in the reactor produces not only heat, which produces steam that operates turbine generators, but also a number of other elements. Some of the uranium 238, which is present but not consumed as part of the fission process, is converted to plutonium in the reactor. When the spent fuel is removed from the reactor, it is a dangerous mix of exceedingly radioactive products, and it must be shielded immediately to avoid severe radiation exposure. After six months or so, the spent fuel has lost enough of its dangerous radioactivity so that it can be carefully handled and shipped. With appropriate shielding and remote-handling procedures, it can then be subjected to chemical processes to extract the plutonium.

Once extracted, plutonium is itself capable of undergoing a nuclear chain reaction. Like U-235, plutonium can explode violently if a quantity exceeding the *critical mass* of the material is compressed together. Or it can sustain a controlled reaction, producing heat but neither exploding nor melting itself and its surroundings in the process. In other words, plutonium is both a nuclear fuel and a nuclear explosive.

As a nuclear fuel, it is not greatly different from the uranium that produced it. It can be assembled into fuel elements and introduced into a nuclear reactor, even the kind of reactor that produced it in the first place. Thus, except for the cost of chemically separating the plutonium from the rest of the spent fuel, the plutonium is a kind of bonus, a usable fuel that is produced by the combustion of another fuel.

---

[1]Spent fuel contains both plutonium and residual enriched uranium, both of which are recovered in reprocessing.

Plutonium separation on a modest scale has been accomplished in many countries and on a larger scale in the United States over a protracted period for its weapons program. But the process has generally been too costly to make plutonium attractive as a processed fuel. A cost that is no obstacle if the objective is weapons or research will be a cost that is excessive if the objective is to produce the cheapest reactor fuel. There is simply not enough experience with large-scale commercial separation of plutonium to allow a confident prediction of whether plutonium will be regularly reprocessed for use as reactor fuel in the next decade.

If it is not, most of the plutonium produced by the nuclear power industries around the world will be bound up with other radioactive wastes accumulating in such forms and locations that it could still be mined and extracted when plutonium reprocessing becomes cheaper or when the price of new uranium fuel rises sufficiently. Small-scale chemical reprocessing, clandestinely or openly, for research or for weapons purposes, would still be a significant problem.

The difference between plutonium and uranium should be kept in mind. The uranium used in today's nuclear power reactors is not capable of being made directly into an explosive. The uranium used as a nuclear fuel in American reactors and in most of the reactors operating in the rest of the world is more than 95 percent U-238, the isotope that does not sustain a chain reaction. Only 2 to 4 percent is U-235, the isotope that sustains a chain reaction. A concentration of 2 to 4 percent is adequate for a controlled heat-producing reaction and therefore adequate for the production of electric energy. But a concentration of more than 20 percent, and preferably 90 percent, is generally considered necessary for the production of an explosive weapon.

If the recycling of plutonium as a nuclear fuel should become generally economic, the quantities of plutonium potentially available will become frighteningly large. Exact synchronization of reprocessing capabilities, country by country, would not be economic, so international as well as internal shipments would become common. The reprocessing locations might well be determined by storage and transport considerations; other considerations would determine the scale and location of fuel-fabrication facilities.

Uranium Enrichment by Gaseous Diffusion. Until recently, enriching uranium to raise the concentration of fissionable U-235 has been an expensive, exceedingly demanding engineering process. It has been economic only on a very large scale and has utilized a technology in which neither

CRITICAL MASS

Unlike gunpowder and TNT, which can be used to make explosives weighing a fraction of an ounce or tens of tons, the quantities of uranium and plutonium that can be used in weapons are measured in units of *critical mass*. It takes a certain minimum quantity of uranium or plutonium to generate an explosive chain reaction. The quantity required depends on the geometry of the fissionable material, its purity, its density, the materials that encase it, and other aspects of the bomb design. But for pure fissionable material in a compact shape, the minimum amount required to generate an explosion can be estimated. Furthermore—and this is what makes critical mass an impressive measure of weapons potential—the minimum amount of uranium or plutonium that is needed to get any significant explosion is enough to produce a very large explosion of the kind that we associate with Hiroshima and Nagasaki. (A bomb has to contain more than one critical mass, but not many times more.) Not any bomb made with the minimum amount of explosive will necessarily have that explosive power. A bomb can be poorly designed, or it can be deliberately designed to

experience nor the technical components are widely distributed around the world. Since World War II, the United States has enriched uranium by a gaseous-diffusion process, in which a uranium gas under pressure is filtered through a membrane that differentially admits the two isotopes, U-235 and U-238, with a small change in their proportions on the other side of the membrane. By putting uranium gas through a *cascade* of more than 1,000 such pressure chambers, the gas can be enriched from the original 0.7 percent to the higher concentration (usually about 3 percent) needed for reactor fuel. Further repetition of the process would raise the U-235 concentration to 10 percent (or 20 or 50 or 90 percent), making it progressively more suitable for use in weapons.

Characteristically, even the smallest practical gaseous-diffusion plant is a huge establishment costing several billion dollars and requiring the equivalent of two or three nuclear power plants to operate it. Further-

release only a fraction of that potential energy. But a well-designed bomb that exploits the full potential power of the fissionable material with minimum waste is a highly destructive atomic weapon yielding energy equivalent to several thousand tons of TNT. Quantities of uranium or plutonium with less than a critical mass will simply not explode at all.

The quantities that constitute a critical mass for uranium 235 and plutonium 239 (and for uranium 233, another possible fissionable reactor product) are different. The amounts generally range from about 5 to 20 kilograms.

With this comparatively unambiguous unit of measure, it is possible to estimate the explosive potential in numbers of critical masses of plutonium produced in a power reactor of some standard size. A modern nuclear power plant of economic size produces around 1,000 megawatts of electric power. (For comparison, total U.S. electric generation capacity is about 500,000 megawatts.) Operating at 70 percent capacity on the average, such a reactor would produce 6 billion kilowatt hours of electricity per year and about 250 kilograms of plutonium. Depending on the purity of the plutonium and the details of design, that would be equivalent to a rate of about one explosive critical mass every two weeks.

more, the metallurgy and engineering of this enrichment process are secret in the United States and would be available to the private economy only under industrial security safeguards. Few countries in the world will find this method economic for enriching uranium for reactor fuel, and none of the less developed countries can find it economic to possess individual uranium-enrichment facilities for at least another generation.

Uranium Enrichment by Gas Centrifuge. The enrichment technology most likely to characterize the medium-term future will be a gas-centrifuge technology that requires less electric power in the separation process and a smaller plant than the gaseous-diffusion method. If a uranium-enrichment plant utilizing gaseous-diffusion technology seems impractical in a country the size of Iran, an enrichment plant utilizing this new centrifuge technology may not seem so. Even if a country the size of Iran would have insufficient demand for the output of a gas-centrifuge facility, it could aspire to an export business in uranium enrichment to help finance its own nuclear independence.

Uranium Enrichment by Laser. In the more distant future, advanced laser beams may be used to separate the U-235 isotopes from the U-238. If that particular technology should emerge, uranium enrichment might become practical on even a very small scale. Even if it was not economic as a source of fuel, it could become a technology capable of producing highly enriched uranium from uranium ore without the heavy expense of a massive isotope-separation plant. Most likely, the laser technology would not be so extraordinarily specialized that it could be construed as prohibited by the Non-Proliferation Treaty.

Uranium Enrichment by Nozzle. West Germany has developed an aerodynamic enrichment process that uses the *Becker nozzle*. An enrichment process based on similar aerodynamic principles is being developed in South Africa. West Germany's recent agreement with Brazil to export nuclear power plants, a reprocessing plant, and a small enrichment plant employing the Becker-nozzle process marks the first time that enrichment technology will be exported.

Proliferation of a nuclear weapons capability on a very broad scale appears likely, even if plutonium reprocessing proves to be unattractively expensive, difficult, or dangerous. The increase of enrichment capabilities utilizing different technologies would entail a different succession of countries over a different time scale. Once a country possesses a capacity for U-235 enrichment, there is no technical obstacle to the use of that capacity for enrichment to weapons-grade proportions. (The cost of enriching to 90 percent U-235, an eminently suitable proportion for efficient weapons use, may not be much more than double the cost of enriching to 3.5 percent or 4 percent.)

Breeder Reactors. Largely because of the worldwide scarcity of readily exploitable high-grade uranium ore, the U.S. government and the governments of France, Britain, Germany, Italy, Japan, and the Soviet Union have been pursuing the development of a reactor that could use the U-238 that constitutes 99.3 percent of natural uranium, not merely the 0.7 percent that is in the form of fissionable U-235. This *breeder reactor* would convert U-238 to fissionable plutonium as a by-product of the generation of heat and electricity and would do so by using plutonium as its fuel. The breeder reactor would actually produce plutonium from U-238 in excess of the plutonium it used for fuel; that is, 1 kilogram of plutonium used as nuclear fuel would not only produce heat for the generation of electricity but would also convert U-238 into more than 1 kilogram of plutonium in the process. In principle, this would make a useful fuel out of all the uranium, not just the U-235. With allowance for some waste, this use of U-238 would increase the energy obtainable from 1 pound of uranium almost a hundredfold and would also make it economic to utilize much-lower-grade ore. Consequently, the supply of uranium would be practically unlimited.

Thorium-Converter Reactors. There is another concept under development that involves introducing the naturally occurring element thorium 232 into a nuclear power reactor, where it would be converted into uranium 233 in much the same way that U-238 is converted into plutonium 239. (This reactor would technically be classified as a *converter* rather than as a breeder because it would not actually produce more U-233 than the fuel being burned.) U-233 is similar to U-235 in that it can be used either as a reactor fuel or as an explosive. Because thorium is comparatively abundant at low cost, the economics of this reactor might be similar to the economics of the plutonium breeder, although the two technologies are somewhat different. Like plutonium, U-233 would be extracted chemically and so would not require expensive isotope separation of the kind required to enrich natural uranium in U-235 content. U-233 is therefore ready to use in the fabrication of either a fuel or an explosive.

Natural-Uranium Reactors. Among several different kinds of power reactors, one more technical concept deserves mention. U-235 at low concentrations requires a *moderator* to slow down neutrons to cause enough fission to sustain the chain reaction. Ordinary water serves the purpose if the concentration of U-235 in the uranium is over 1 percent. U.S. reactors typically use a concentration of around 2 to 3 percent U-235. If *heavy water* is used instead, a chain reaction can be sustained in a reactor with natural uranium in which the concentration is only 0.7 percent U-235.[2] A power reactor of that kind has been developed by the Canadian government, and such reactors are in operation in Canada. It was with a research reactor built on this principle that India (with Canadian assis-

---

[2]Heavy water is a variety of water formed with deuterium, an isotope of hydrogen with twice the atomic weight of ordinary hydrogen.

tance) produced the plutonium for its recent "peaceful" explosion.

This power reactor, known as CANDU (for "Canadian deuterium uranium"), bypasses the expensive enrichment process but entails an expensive moderator, heavy water. Several nations may elect the Canadian technology and develop their own capacity for the production of the necessary heavy water. (Argentina has a pilot plant for heavy water and a natural-uranium power reactor.) For various technical reasons, the CANDU technology is somewhat better for production of weapons-grade plutonium than the light-water reactors used and exported by the United States. The CANDU reactor does not need to be shut down when its fuel is replaced; the CANDU technology makes it comparatively easy to extract some fuel that has been burning a short time and therefore contains less of the undesired plutonium isotopes and hazardous fission products.

NUCLEAR REACTORS AND WEAPONS PROGRAMS

Acquisition of a major nuclear establishment need no longer be considered a suspect activity. The immense programs announced by the governments of Brazil and Iran to build approximately 10,000 megawatts of installed nuclear electric power during the coming decade or so, with facilities for the processing of nuclear fuels, are sufficiently justified on economic grounds; they can hardly be construed as merely an enormous camouflage for a nuclear weapons program, however much those countries might also desire a nuclear weapons capability.

Testing an actual weapon without being detected would be difficult.[3] But on a standby basis, without using plutonium, government arsenals could contain all the components of a plutonium bomb ready to be assembled, for addition to a weapons stockpile, for demonstration, or for a test program to help select the best weapons design. It is generally expected that after such preparation, the time needed to produce a finished plutonium bomb would probably be measured in weeks or days, rather than in months.

It would not be difficult to hide or disguise the laser-enrichment process if it were used in violation of treaties or other agreements. Again,

---

[3]Testing an explosive with a bare minimum of instrumentation, not for research, but to verify that it detonates and to estimate its explosive yield within useful limits, might be done anonymously but not undetectably on the open seas.

there may be no particular need to violate the treaty until a government finds itself in a military emergency. The difference is one of lead time, and a country that feels the need to abrogate the treaty will need to do so only a little more quickly in order to activate its nuclear mobilization plans.

Some governments express interest in the use of nuclear explosives for nonmilitary purposes. The Indian government announced that its detonation of a nuclear device in 1974 was a test of a "peaceful nuclear explosive" of a kind that might be useful in excavation or construction or some project that could use a large, concentrated source of explosive energy. Although there are bound to be differences in detail between an explosive designed for delivery against a military target and an explosive designed for peaceful excavation, the fundamental explosion is the same. Studies in the United States and elsewhere suggest there are few (if any) practical applications of this kind of explosion. The U.S. government questions the economic worth of such "peaceful" uses; however, the Soviet Union expresses official interest in the nonweapons use of nuclear explosives.

THE CERTAINTY: WORLDWIDE CAPABILITY FOR NUCLEAR WEAPONS

The engineering facilities required to design and build a plutonium bomb generally require no more than a building of modest size and the kind of equipment that can be freely obtained in the open market. People with the scientific and technical training to use the publicly available information about how to fabricate a nuclear bomb and people with the engineering and other skills to participate in actual design and construction are not scarce. They reside in dozens of countries. Although there is no master list of who they are, many among them could easily be located, by their own government or by any other government, in the event their services were desired in a project to design or fabricate a bomb.[4]

---

[4]See Mason Willrich and Theodore B. Taylor, *Nuclear Theft: Risks and Safeguards* (Cambridge, Mass.: Ballinger Publishing Company, 1974), especially pages 20–21. Hans A. Bethe, B. L. Cohen, and Richard Wilson state: "It is clear that any nation with a moderate industrial capacity can make a bomb—or even several—without outside aid." (India made one.) "The United States took three years of development; now that everything is public knowledge, it is simpler." Commenting that Willrich and Taylor may have overemphasized the ease of constructing nuclear weapons, they assert that "at least six persons, highly skilled in very different technologies, would be required to do so, even for a crude weapon." (Statement presented to the National Council of Churches, January 28, 1976.)

There is disagreement among experts about how easy it is to make an effective nuclear bomb if the plutonium or the enriched uranium is available only to scientists and engineers who have no direct weapons-design or -testing experience. The fact is that nearly every government and, in particular, its armed forces, security forces, or nuclear affairs ministry, will be going through a decade of planning and anticipating the development of nuclear technology. Governments will recognize that they will soon possess adequate quantities of fissionable materials and some experience in handling them. They will recognize that in other countries the study of nuclear explosives is generally not suppressed. They will have time to train scientists and engineers who could, as a precautionary measure, prepare plans for the assembly of nuclear weapons in some future emergency. Most universities in the Western world will provide the basic nuclear physics and engineering to pupils from any country so long as they are qualified and can pay the tuition.

The question of whether a country has nuclear weapons will then be answered, not with a yes or a no, but with a mobilization schedule: the estimated elapsed time from the decision to assemble weapons to the possession of the first, the second, the tenth, the hundredth weapon.

In the event of revolution, civil war, or military coup d'etat, individuals or groups other than national governments could gain possession of nuclear materials. They could fall into unknown hands or become the property of a successor government that chose not to recognize certain treaty commitments if the previous government had been party to the Non-Proliferation Treaty.

Whether governments in today's international climate will actually assemble bombs in the near future is therefore only one question. The worst consequence of the increased possession of nuclear weapons would be the actual use of nuclear weapons. Threats to use them, backed by demonstrated capabilities, would be grave enough.

The worldwide spread of nuclear reactors for power appears to be nearly inevitable. A severe accident might slow this development, and some present uncertainties of cost and technology may be resolved in a way that retards that development. But it is not likely that the building of reactors will cease. The consequent increased threat of nuclear accidents, terrorism, or war appears to be similarly inevitable.

Almost as certain is some spread of research reactors, enrichment facilities, and reprocessing plants. These, not power installations, pose the gravest threat of providing materials for nuclear weapons.

NUCLEAR REACTORS
AND WORLDWIDE ENERGY NEEDS

It must be recognized that the strongest driving force behind nuclear development is economic, not military. The suddenness with which the world petroleum market changed its character and the suddenness with which petroleum prices rose to double-digit dollar levels dramatized but did not create the fundamental, long-term problem. That problem is two-fold. First, the world's petroleum resources will not sustain the world's economic development beyond the rest of this century. Second, most of the world's petroleum reserves are controlled by a very few governments, most of them in the Middle East.

The traditional forms of liquid petroleum and natural gas cannot be relied on to meet the world's burgeoning demand for energy for more than another generation. The continued need for petroleum for liquid fuel and other purposes besides the production of steam to make electric power will further aggravate the scarcity of petroleum as a source of pure energy.

With double-digit dollar prices per barrel of oil, the costs of nuclear power plants in highly developed countries appear to be both economically competitive with oil-fired generating plants and a prudent hedge against higher oil and coal prices and scarcities in the future. (Cartels and embargoes may not be inevitable, but their absence cannot be taken for granted in making long-term investments in generating capacity.) For most of the less developed countries, which have small electric power systems, nuclear power plants are not yet cheaper than oil-fired generating plants, but this situation will change in time.

This worldwide harnessing of nuclear energy for electricity will therefore be motivated primarily by the economic advantages of nuclear energy, by the strategic importance of reduced dependence on nonnuclear fuels, and by a desire to stay abreast of developing nuclear technology. It need not reflect an immediate interest in nuclear weapons.

U.S. INFLUENCE ON WORLDWIDE
NUCLEAR ENERGY DEVELOPMENT

It is no longer within the power of the United States, if indeed it ever was, to prevent the rest of the world from moving toward nuclear electric power. However much influence the United States can have over the shape and character of the world's nuclear development, it cannot stop

that development. Even if the United States were prepared to forgo nuclear energy at home, out of a preference for increased mining and combustion of coal and other fossil fuels, it could not prevent the spread of nuclear reactors throughout both the developed and the less developed worlds.

The United States no longer possesses anything resembling a monopoly on reactor technology. There are many industrial countries capable of producing and exporting reactors and reactor fuel, and the industrial processes by which material for nuclear explosives can be obtained from the reactor fuel cycle. Nor is the United States the only industrial country capable of developing and utilizing or exporting the equipment and technology for plutonium recycling. For example, several other countries are developing and experimenting with breeder reactors.

Ironically, the proliferation of nuclear weapons *capacity* would not be contrary to the letter or the spirit of the Non-Proliferation Treaty. Article 4 of that treaty not only preserves "the inalienable right of all the Parties to the Treaty to develop research, production and use of nuclear energy for peaceful purposes without discrimination." It also states that "Parties to the Treaty in a position to do so shall also cooperate in contributing alone or together with other states or international organizations to the further development of the applications of nuclear energy for peaceful purposes, especially in the territories of non-nuclear-weapon States Parties to the Treaty, with due consideration for the needs for the developing areas of the world."

If the United States attempted to embargo or otherwise to hinder the export of materials and equipment and technology subject to the safeguards negotiated under that treaty, it would jeopardize and very likely destroy whatever legal and diplomatic basis it has for negotiating nuclear safeguards.*

NUCLEAR REACTORS AND NATIONAL SECURITY

Until recently, the greatest national security problem, nuclear proliferation, was seen almost exclusively as a problem of curbing the temptations of national governments around the world to obtain a nuclear explosive capability of military significance, either for outright military use or to enhance national prestige and bargaining power. The Non-Proliferation Treaty that was so carefully negotiated and that has now been, or is being, accepted by approximately 100 countries reflects that

*See memorandum by LINCOLN GORDON, page 70.

view. It is also true that until recently large-scale use of nuclear power to meet the electricity needs of most countries seemed distant and problematical. But events have overtaken both these views.

For the past decade, U.S. efforts to cope with nuclear proliferation have been focused on the Non-Proliferation Treaty. Henceforth, the treaty must be part of much more complicated legal and diplomatic safeguards upon the "peaceful" uses of nuclear energy.

Recent events have not removed the strong inhibitory effect of the Non-Proliferation Treaty and a multitude of agreements, contractual arrangements, alliance obligations, and other constraints. Nations, merely because they are capable of assembling weapons in an emergency, will not necessarily do so or threaten to do so. But nations will have mobilization bases that could be activated to produce nuclear explosives; furthermore, they will be known to have them. It the event of war or emergency, those nuclear weapons potentials will play a central role in the plans and expectations of all parties to the emergency. Plutonium-reprocessing facilities or uranium-enrichment facilities, even the power reactors themselves, would be sensitive military targets in the event of war or preemptive attack. On the one hand, they represent the source of nuclear explosive material (other than fissionable material already on hand or assembled into weapons); on the other hand, the chemical-reprocessing facilities and the reactors could be sources of deadly radioactive materials if successfully attacked with that in view.

It must also be recognized that a significant fraction of the world's governments will probably not sign and ratify the Non-Proliferation Treaty. In addition to France and the People's Republic of China, which have made it clear that they have no intention of becoming parties to the treaty (and which, had they joined, would have joined in the category of nuclear weapons states), more than two dozen nations may in the end decline to participate. Argentina, Brazil, and Chile may remain outside; so may India, Pakistan, Bangladesh, Israel, Saudi Arabia, South Africa, Spain, Portugal, and other countries in Africa, the Middle East, and the Caribbean.

Although the United States can extol the Non-Proliferation Treaty, it cannot deny other nations the right to make up their own minds about whether participation in the treaty is economically advantageous, militarily reassuring, diplomatically wise, and morally virtuous. More important, the United States must be as interested in nuclear developments within the countries that are not parties to the treaty as in developments within participating countries.

CHANGING MILITARY PRIORITIES

U.S. military planning has devoted much attention to the avoidance of nuclear proliferation. A dominant feature of alliance arrangements has been assurance to other nations that they do not need independent nuclear capabilities. Security guarantees from the United States have been conditional on acceptance of a nonnuclear status by other countries. A major purpose of stationing troops overseas (in Europe and the Far East) had always been to reduce incentives in allied countries to proceed with their own nuclear weapons programs. The SALT agreements with the Soviet Union and the earlier Nuclear Test Ban Treaty were motivated by the need to bring nuclear weapons under control and to help generate a greater willingness around the world to abstain from national nuclear weapons programs.

But there is little sign that the $100 billion or more that the United States spends annually on its military establishment is directly concerned with a worldwide nuclear economy and its weapons potential. The security implications of these global trends are enormous and deserve careful attention. They are of a magnitude that might be expected to command an increased part of the resources the United States puts into its national defense structure, but there is no sign yet that they do.

There are reasons why such a drastic change in the nature of U.S. national security problems is not yet reflected in national defense programs and policies. It is difficult to know how the nation might restructure its spending and its forces to prepare for that further complication. Furthermore, the traditional way in which this country's defense problems have been handled—with massively expensive traditional military forces—may not be the best approach to these problems.

A third consideration is that until now the United States has been concerned with making the Non-Proliferation Treaty and related efforts succeed. For that purpose, it is important to credit the treaty with being a major safeguard against that multitude of potential nuclear dangers. To be preparing, visibly and energetically, for a world of nuclear proliferation while attempting to negotiate the Non-Proliferation Treaty as a major bulwark against the emerging peril could have put the United States in a seemingly contradictory position that surely would have undermined its efforts on behalf of nonproliferation diplomacy.

It is not clear just where, among U.S. agencies, responsibility for coping with the kind of nuclear threats suggested by the term *terrorism* will lie. Terrorism may epitomize the kind of military problem that will arise in the next twenty years, although terrorism may not necessarily occur in its more familiar forms, such as hijackings and the taking of hostages.

Nuclear military threats between governments may take on many of the characteristics of terrorist threats. If restrained by the Non-Proliferation Treaty, the military forces of most countries are not explicitly built around nuclear weapons or nuclear capabilities. Therefore, military crises in such countries may well take a terrorist form. As weapons of last resort, nuclear explosives may be brought to bear to forestall military disaster. Vague nuclear threats may be used to deter imminent attack. Demonstrations of possession may be part of intimidation or of deterrent response to intimidation. It is instructive to remember that the only use of nuclear weapons in warfare was by a government that possessed *only two weapons,* the reliability of which could not be assured.

The only government that has exploded nuclear weapons in warfare wanted maximum shock effect and, having considered a variety of alternatives ranging from demonstration on a deserted island to a use against military facilities, ultimately decided, in the interest of stopping a war, to drop the first bomb and the second on military-industrial-population centers.*

In thinking about the future meaning of nuclear terrorism, it is instructive to reflect on the frequency with which national military forces engage in the overthrow of civilian governments or in civil war and even on the frequency with which the armed forces of countries are split into opposing factions. Moreover, the technical knowledge to assemble a nuclear explosive device will not be confined to national armed services. The theft or capture of nuclear materials (in storage or in transit) by revolutionaries, terrorists, criminals, or even armed forces during a civil war or a coup d'etat will be a frightening possibility. It may become an occasional reality.

It is not clear what the U.S. military establishment should do in anticipation of these possibilities. The wisdom of minimal involvement may have to be weighed against the necessity for some kind of vigorous collective action.

But there is one line of policy that may need to be even more vigorously pursued in the future. It is the policy of keeping nuclear weapons as separate as possible from any other kinds of weapons, of treating any possibility of their use as the highest presidential responsibility, of treating nuclear weapons as uniquely in need of special efforts at arms control, and generally of surrounding them with awe and with a sense that temptations to use them ought to be resisted. Despite U.S. deterrent reliance on

*See memorandum by LINCOLN GORDON, page 71.

nuclear weapons and the threat of using them, American presidents have always vigorously supported this policy.

Terrorist activities in recent years suggest the precarious state of a world in which weapons of dramatically enhanced potency and frightfulness might be available to political movements or to nonnational groups and organizations. It may be fallacious to suppose that the various groups and individuals that have practiced terrorism in recent years are harbingers of the nuclear terrorism that might emerge in ten or fifteen years. However popular plutonium bomb technology may become in the 1990s, it will continue to be far more demanding than anything used by present-day terrorists. But the terrorists of the 1970s probably do not exhaust the array of potential private and political organizations or motives that will need to concern us.

The proliferation of nuclear mobilization bases and even of assembled weapons at the disposal of scores of national governments is an alarming prospect. However, there is at least the *possibility* that the possession of nuclear weapons in a world in which other countries, both friends and enemies, also possess a nuclear capability will induce caution. A highly explosive world may be a world in which governments tread with care and avoid explosive confrontations.

There appear to be strong reasons why the United States is not yet in a position to participate in a universal declaration against first use of nuclear weapons. The United States has defense commitments to various allies who, correctly or not, believe that a willingness on the part of this country to introduce nuclear weapons into conflict is a necessary threat to deter nonnuclear attack. But ideas such as the universal declaration of no first use will deserve reconsideration as the nuclear world becomes a reality.*

NEED FOR PLANNING

There is no straightforward military protection against these forthcoming dangers. Nor is there any foreign or commercial policy that can arrest the development of the capability to construct nuclear weapons.[5]

---

[5]It might be argued that U.S. coal reserves could supply the world's needs for more than 100 years and that a world coal economy based on U.S. coal is as feasible as the recent world economy based on OPEC oil. But collective experience with OPEC may be sufficient reason for other nations not to favor this possibility, and in any

*See memorandum by JAMES T. HILL, Jr., page 71.

This does not mean, however, that no military, diplomatic, or technical means of national safeguards will be found.

The United States needs to begin planning those safeguards now. Furthermore, it is necessary to begin planning with other countries for coping with possible nuclear emergencies. If skillfully done, this planning could help to develop and to reinforce a common interest in safeguarding against the more frightening contingencies.

There are at least four critical areas of American policy in which planning must start to cope with these developments. One is national defense, together with U.S. policy toward the military use of nuclear weapons. A second is foreign policy: negotiating safeguards against nuclear terror and disaster through persistent, painful dedication to building effective international institutions. A third is technology, both of nuclear energy and of surveillance necessary to monitor nuclear materials being produced, utilized, and stored around the world to guard against the likelihood of theft, sabotage, and accident. The fourth area—essential to the first three—is energy, especially nuclear energy and all its ramifications.

One does not have to be an alarmist to observe that a world in which a large number of governments have the physical ability to acquire nuclear explosives on short notice will be a world with new tensions and dangers. One can speculate on whether a multifaceted balance of terror will induce universal caution, inhibit international violence, and even bring about a precarious measure of safety. Not everything that *can* happen always *does* happen, and to recognize the potential peril does not require a corresponding abandonment of hope. But the focus of this country's nuclear anxieties in the decades to come will surely change from the exclusive East-West nuclear rivalry of recent decades. *

---

event, a U.S. effort to promote its own coal exports as a complete substitute for nuclear energy would be suspect as well as unappealing. Furthermore, the required expansion of coal output in the United States for domestic use will tax the industry's capability to grow.

*See memorandum by JAMES T. HILL, Jr., page 71.

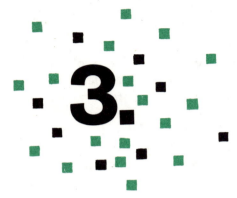

Needs, Plans, and Choices:
What Can the United States Do
to Lessen the Risks?

THE PLUTONIUM ECONOMY and a world of nuclear mobilization bases are still some distance away. They will emerge in about twenty years. But plans, decisions, and commitments must be made immediately; and these will determine the institutional setting, the safeguards, and the diplomatic context that could shape the plutonium economy. Hence, the problems are simultaneously distant and urgent. The development of policies to cope with them cannot wait.

What is striking is how little of the U.S. government's visible long-term defense planning is concerned with a world of widespread nuclear potential. New weapons such as the B-1 bomber or the Trident submarine have such long lead times between commissioning and completion that they have to be decided on a decade in advance and evaluated in terms of their contribution during a period that will arrive fifteen or twenty years from now.[1] If, therefore, any new military capabilities are going to be needed to cope with the contingencies that arise in a nuclear world, it is not too early to begin giving them serious consideration.

---

[1]For discussion of these issues, see *Congressional Decision Making for National Security* (1974).

At this point, channeling funds into military forces would be wasteful. To appear to be making vigorous military preparations, as though a nuclear weapons capability is being taken for granted in most countries of the world, could conflict with U.S. diplomatic efforts in support of nonproliferation. But it is essential now to explore what plans and preparations we *should* be making. The United States cannot afford to ignore what goes on in the nuclear energy industry abroad.

The complex dangers posed by a worldwide nuclear economy should receive high priority in American national security planning. The danger of intercontinental nuclear warfare has been unique in the national security attention it has deservedly received for a quarter of a century. In another dozen years, it will begin to be rivaled by the lesser but nevertheless immense danger of a worldwide capacity for nuclear warfare or nuclear mischief.*

U.S. NUCLEAR ENERGY DEBATE: FALSE CHOICES AND REAL CHOICES

The many hazards associated with nuclear energy, especially with nuclear explosives, are enough to make any thoughtful person wonder whether, despite the world's need for new sources of energy, it might be better for mankind if nuclear technology could be suppressed and forgotten. A world economy charging toward a fuel shortage with no immediate relief in sight may be less frightening than a world economy powered by the fuel equivalent of millions of nuclear bombs. When the problem of radioactive wastes and the possibility of ordinary accidents are added, it is no wonder that concerned individuals are asking whether the world is obliged to imperil itself in this way.

If the United States were the only nation in the world in need of nuclear energy, it might indeed be wise for this country to reappraise its course. But this is not the case. It is simply not within the power of the United States to turn the world away from nuclear energy. Nuclear energy and the plutonium economy will almost certainly develop regardless of whatever decision the United States reaches about its future energy sources. Removing the United States from the plutonium economy will not protect this country from its hazards.

There will be no easy solutions to the security problems associated with the worldwide development of nuclear energy. But without vigorous U.S. participation in that development, there may be no solutions at all. We believe there is no choice. Only by continuing to exercise leadership in the worldwide development of atomic energy can the United States hope to influence the way the world's nuclear economy is safeguarded. To withdraw U.S. support from peaceful nuclear developments abroad or to renounce nuclear energy and suppress its technological development in this country would be to abandon whatever moderating influence the United States can hope to exercise through continued cooperation and leadership.

Energy Isolationism: Not an Option. Nuclear isolationism is simply not an available option for the United States. The question is not whether the benefits are worth the risks. The United States cannot eliminate the risks by forgoing the benefits. Worse, this country can lose what leadership it has in world nuclear development by turning its back on that development and by failing to live up to the spirit of the Non-Proliferation Treaty.

There is equal danger from another kind of isolationism. If this country belittles or ignores the risks of nuclear proliferation and develops an energy policy that is insulated from world developments and focused exclusively on American needs, it will weaken many of its allies, jeopardize its relations with them, and lose the opportunity to have an effective voice in the nuclear development of the rest of the world. Energy independence for the United States will be worth little if it becomes energy isolationism. Even strategic insulation against potentially unfriendly oil-producing countries will be worse than self-defeating if it leaves Japan and Western Europe more dependent. An energy strategy based solely on U.S. needs would totally disregard the fact that the world is going to become a harder, not an easier, place for a rich industrial nation to survive in alone.

The question of whether plutonium can be economically extracted from spent reactor fuel and recycled into the reactor as a partial substitute for uranium fuel is a controversial issue. There is disagreement about a purely economic question: Will plutonium, as a reactor fuel, be competitive with uranium; if so, how soon will the cost of plutonium separation, compared with the costs of uranium ore and of uranium enrichment, make it competitive? And there is dispute about values: If we prefer *not* to live in a plutonium economy because of the dangers associated with plutonium, what will it cost to forgo the recycling of plutonium, and what is it worth?

Fuel costs presently account for about 20 percent of the cost of nuclear energy per kilowatt hour. If recycling were absolutely free, the cost of nuclear power could perhaps be 4 percent less than it is now.

But because recycling will not be free, the saving is likely to be no more than 1 or 2 percent.

As the United States weighs the wisdom of forgoing any fuel economies of plutonium recycling and paying whatever the costs of uranium fuels will be in the future, a discouraging fact becomes apparent. Most other countries in the world will evaluate the economies and the potential dangers quite differently. The United States, with its elevated standard of living compared with the less developed world, may well judge the hazards of chemical reprocessing very differently from countries that expect to suffer far more from poverty and economic backwardness than from radiological dangers.

If plutonium extraction becomes common in the rest of the world, most of the benefits that might be hoped for from a deliberate suppression of plutonium extraction in this country will simply not materialize. Forgoing any possible economic advantages of plutonium recycling in this country would not prevent plutonium from becoming accessible to unauthorized use elsewhere in the world. It would, instead, leave the United States with the additional problem of persuading poorer countries and countries less likely to consider themselves unreliable where plutonium is concerned that they should forgo those benefits. The United States might have to negotiate arrangements by which this country and a few other nations would offer to subsidize the purchase of increasingly expensive uranium fuels for countries that possessed no other fuel.

Failure to expand the U.S. uranium-enrichment capability may have two other serious economic consequences. First, there is the possibility of a shortage of reactor fuel, a shortage that might particularly inhibit long-term contracts for nuclear fuel with foreign purchases of electric power reactors. Second, the United States will lose nuclear fuel markets to increasing competition from foreign suppliers. In 1975, the United States possessed more than 90 percent of the uranium-enrichment capability in the non-Soviet world; by the mid-1980s, several projected enrichment facilities in Europe and Japan might be producing half as much or more.

Frustrating and unsatisfying as it will be to participate in world nuclear diplomacy, the alternative to even precarious and incomplete success will be disastrous. Most, if not all, of the dangers arising from the increase of nuclear power and the attendant production of plutonium will have to be lived with regardless of whether plutonium is produced by power reactors within the boundaries of the continental United States. The development of nuclear energy and the proliferation of national nuclear weapons capabilities around the world will not be stopped by any American resolve to forgo nuclear energy. Even the threat of plutonium bombs in the hands of terrorists would not be much affected by the absence of a plutonium fuel industry in this country.

Compared with the more familiar forms of terrorism, obtaining a nuclear bomb would be exceedingly complex and demanding. But merely denying a domestic source of the critical nuclear materials to an organization capable of the rest of the task would not increase the difficulty very much. Bringing the nuclear material into the country would be a comparatively minor problem for any organization able to acquire the materials, produce an explosive device, and make political or criminal use of it. The problem is real. The solution offered by some—forgoing nuclear energy at home while its development burgeons abroad and even refusing to meet U.S. treaty commitments—would be a futile kind of isolationism.

The same is true of the problem of nuclear wastes. People are gravely concerned because the fission products of nuclear reactors will remain dangerously radioactive for years. But in the perspective of millenia, what happens to the earth will be only marginally affected by what happens in this portion of the North American continent. The United States could avoid a local problem of waste management by doing without nuclear energy, but it could not save the earth from having to accommodate nuclear wastes during the coming centuries.

Nothing could be more self-defeating than an attempt to escape the problems of nuclear energy development by denying ourselves that development within the United States. Unless a way can be found to detach the United States from the planet Earth and put it into independent orbit around the sun, it cannot escape the perils attending the worldwide development of nuclear energy by choosing to remain isolated from that development.

DEVELOPING SUPPLY TO REDUCE THE RISKS

The United States still has important leverage on world nuclear developments through its production of nuclear fuel and its leading but not dominant position in nuclear power technologies. It now possesses about 90 percent of the free world's capacity to enrich uranium for processing into fuel assemblies for nuclear reactors, but that capacity is substantially committed by contract and is inadequate to meet the potential demand of new reactors being built or planned. Thus, the U.S. government is not in a position to wield much bargaining power over the worldwide development of nuclear energy through the supply of nuclear fuel. Countries dependent on imports of nuclear fuel will need to be assured that there is an adequate supply of fuels for their current reactor operations and even for stockpiling abroad.

Crucial decisions will hinge on just how scarce or plentiful uranium ore is in the United States and around the world and just what the costs of extraction will be. The need for improved estimates through exploration is urgent. **We recommend that the United States vigorously pursue its program of exploration of uranium deposits within this country and develop cooperative methods for estimating supplies of uranium ore in other parts of the world.** This will make it easier to estimate the future demand for technologies, such as breeder reactors or plutonium recycling, in an open, multilateral process that takes adequate account of the needs of other countries. **In addition, we urge that all present restrictions on the importation and use of foreign uranium be immediately removed.**

GOVERNMENT'S ROLE

A major unresolved issue is the proper role of the U.S. government in the ownership or control of production facilities for nuclear fuel, including uranium enrichment, chemical reprocessing of spent fuel for the extraction of plutonium and residual uranium, and exploration of uranium ore reserves.

Until now, all uranium enrichment in the United States has been done by the federal government, using facilities originally intended for the development of weapons programs, but future development of uranium-enrichment capabilities will be for power reactors. Presidential policy in recent years has been that private industry rather than the federal government should finance the next expansion of uranium-enrichment capacity. To date, Congress, the executive branch, and private industry have not completed the legal arrangements for that next step. There are a number of reasons for this, including the likelihood that a facility costing several billion dollars with an expected productive lifetime of twenty years or more would soon become obsolete because it would have to compete with the new gas-centrifuge technology and possibly with a laser technology, both of which are expected to lower the price of enriched uranium.

It has become clear that an early expansion of uranium-enrichment capacity will depend on the traditional technology of gaseous diffusion and that private companies will not finance this development without comprehensive federal loan guarantees of a kind that may not be forthcoming. **But it is urgent to proceed with the next stage of expansion using the older technology. We expect government assumption of financial risks to be comprehensive whether this interim stage is conducted publicly or privately.*** What makes the matter serious is that the supply of nuclear fuel is likely to be one of the few potential inducements that the U.S. government may have at its disposal during the coming decade in helping to shape the development of the world nuclear fuel cycle. We believe that private industry in cooperation with government should competitively develop the forthcoming centrifuge process of uranium enrichment.

NRC has the power to license or to withhold license from the reprocessing of spent fuel. It is within NRC's authority to determine whether the process in general is too hazardous to license or, alternatively, to be prepared to license reprocessing plants and to scrutinize each application individually. NRC will take into account the radiological hazards of the industrial process itself and the transport and security problems associated with the production of potentially explosive plutonium.

NRC's announced policy is to postpone the determination of a final policy on the licensing of chemical reprocessing while allowing one newly constructed reprocessing facility to operate, presumably as a source of valuable experience. Like other pending decisions about nuclear energy, this one is charged with foreign policy implications. *A "go" decision by NRC would be a strong signal to the rest of the world that plutonium recycling is a part of the nuclear future.* If plutonium recycling occurs on a commercial scale worldwide, the plutonium economy will emerge, and some of the objections to development of the breeder reactor will be eliminated. A "go" decision by NRC would also put the United States in the position of continued engineering development, so that this country might take a lead in institutionalizing plutonium recycling in international ways that would be less perilous than separate national recycling facilities. For example, the U.S. government might then propose that spent fuels be reprocessed at several locations around the world under multinational auspices, perhaps even governed by new treaty arrangements, rather than at the national level within individual countries.

A negative decision by NRC would slow and discourage the development of the plutonium economy.* It would signal that the process was considered too hazardous or too expensive. It would presumably also signal that the United States would not take initiatives with respect to the

*See memoranda by LINCOLN GORDON, page 70.

location and institutional arrangements for plutonium recycling abroad and would not be developing the reprocessing technology for export, except as a longer-term preparation for the time when the plutonium breeder reactor may become economic.

We make no pretense that there is a correct decision that can be anticipated before NRC gathers the evidence and experimental data, hears testimony, and weighs all the issues. There are crucial issues of domestic security, economics, and public health that cannot be wholly subordinated to foreign policy and external national security. There are matters of national security and foreign policy in other countries that ought to have substantial weight in any decision, whether that decision is to proceed rapidly, to proceed cautiously, to postpone reprocessing for further consideration, or to postpone it indefinitely. Furthermore, the economics of reprocessing spent fuel is very much bound up in the economics of uranium enrichment, the economics of exploration for uranium ore, and the ultimate transition from scarce U-235 to some more abundant nuclear fuel, whether it is plutonium, some combination of plutonium and thorium converted to U-233, or ultimately some controlled process of nuclear fusion.

What needs emphasis is that a policy decision on reprocessing spent fuel and extracting plutonium is of enormous consequence both for the domestic economy and domestic society and for U.S. foreign policy and the foreign policy and national security of other countries.

In *Achieving Energy Independence,* this Committee noted that government might have to assume some of the risks of energy development and that it might be necessary with respect to new energy sources to establish new organizations for transforming government pilot developments into commercial endeavors: "This effort might embody roles and functions paralleling the Reconstruction Finance Corporation of the 1930s." In supporting production of synthetic fuels by private industry, we observed that "contracting for and disposing of these fuels could become an essential government responsibility." There is a compelling need for institutions to deal with nuclear fuels, especially in international trade. Nuclear fuels pose unique problems, both of security and of safety, and the United States has powerful reasons to influence the way these problems are handled throughout the world.

We recommend that the nuclear fuel industry be treated as one in which the sharing of responsibility by private and government institutions be considered particularly appropriate. New institutions for the financing, ownership, and management of many kinds of nuclear facilities and for safeguarding nuclear materials will prove unavoidable. The United States should be particularly interested in collaborative institutions by which the eighteen IEA nations can better coordinate their energy programs and develop their energy resources.

We have too little experience with the new way in which the U.S. government has been organized for the conduct of nuclear affairs, especially NRC, to judge its effectiveness. But the test of whether these new arrangements can work is likely to be the test of whether domestic and foreign policy can be brought together in the new decision mechanism.

NUCLEAR DIPLOMACY: BARGAINING FOR SAFEGUARDS

For more than two decades, the United States has played a leading role in the international development of peaceful nuclear energy. This policy has always been a gamble. By contributing, participating, and cooperating, the United States has attempted to maintain an ability to guide and influence that nuclear development toward world safety and toward minimizing the proliferation of nuclear weapons and their use. During the past decade, the United States made a substantial, if incompletely successful, effort to bind together most of the nations of the world in the Treaty on the Non-Proliferation of Nuclear Weapons. In that treaty, nations not only committed themselves to abstain from developing weapons or helping other nations to develop them but also submitted their peaceful nuclear activities to safeguards and inspection by a commonly supported international agency. In return, the United States committed itself to facilitate the development abroad of peaceful uses of nuclear energy. This, too, was a gamble, based on the belief that more could be accomplished for both world safety and American security through American cooperation in restrained nuclear development than through any unilateral American effort to suppress a technology that could at best be delayed. We believe it was a wise gamble. We also believe there was really no choice.

There is the possibility that the hazards of the plutonium economy can be minimized in the years to come. There is the possibility that the accumulation of fissionable materials that could quickly be assembled into bombs can be inhibited and that adequate safeguards against theft or diversion of fissionable material from legitimate uses can be devised. There is the possibility that something can be done to assure governments that other governments are abstaining from the assembly of nuclear explosives. But the United States will have little or no influence on these matters if it turns its back on those developments, gives up its leadership in them, and suppresses even the peaceful development of nuclear energy at home.

The key point for the United States is that there is an essential diplomatic role for the federal government and a parallel essential productive and commercial role for private enterprise. Coupling and coordinating these two roles is an immediate challenge. Overseas diplomacy cannot be the direct responsibility of private enterprise, nor can private enterprise be expected, in the development of a multibillion-dollar nuclear industry, to cultivate foreign interest in special multinational safeguard arrangements on its own initiative, especially if those arrangements may involve some economic contribution or special financial participation by the federal government. It is in the direct interest of the U.S. government to see that the resources are available with which it may conduct its peaceful nuclear diplomacy abroad.

The Non-Proliferation Treaty is one of many formal arrangements that will help to structure and guide worldwide nuclear development. Multinational arrangements for reprocessing spent fuel or for enriching uranium could represent another important step in this development. International arrangements for the storage, the disposal, and especially, the safe shipment of radioactive wastes need to be negotiated. There is need for international collaboration to deal with the loss or theft of fissionable materials, and there may have to be international cooperation to deal with accidents to shipments of waste or to reactors. Formal arrangements, analogous to those that the U.S. government has from time to time negotiated in respect to aircraft hijacking, are needed to cope with the possibility of nuclear terrorism.

In some of these arrangements, it is important to get the most nearly universal participation that can be negotiated. Others, such as multinational facilities for waste disposal or the reprocessing of spent fuel, can be organized regionally. A major obstacle to the necessary diplomatic flexibility in the next ten years is that the Non-Proliferation Treaty itself, various bilateral commitments and promises, and resolutions taken at the five-year review conference under the treaty in 1974 impose some obligation on the United States to give nations that sign and ratify the treaty favorable treatment in its export policies, export financing, and provision of technical assistance. To some extent, this was a natural matter of safeguarding nuclear technology by attempting to restrict its spread to those countries that committed themselves to abstain from weapons development and that submitted to IAEA inspection. To some extent, it was a conscious inducement, an offer of favorable treatment to nations that might otherwise have decided to stay out of the treaty.

We strongly recommend that the United States negotiate with all nuclear-supplying countries, including those that are not signatories of the Treaty on the Non-Proliferation of Nuclear Weapons, to attach common International Atomic Energy Agency safeguards on all sales to all countries. Such safeguards should be more stringent than they are now and should apply not only to the actual facilities and materials exported but also to any indigenous production of nuclear facilities or materials.

IAEA safeguards are an important step toward controlling nuclear dangers, but their effectiveness should not be overstated. Even the term *safeguards* is misleading; current IAEA safeguards amount only to inspection, surveillance, and record keeping. Safeguards apply only to civilian nuclear power installations, and they do not restrain a country from openly making bombs or from having fissionable materials usable in bombs. If a country violates safeguard agreements, IAEA can only sound an alarm. There is no established mechanism for dealing with a country or individual that has broken a safeguard agreement, and no signatory to the Non-Proliferation Treaty has proposed such a mechanism. IAEA can only alert the United States and other countries to problems that in the end must be dealt with by political solutions.

The primary institutional safeguards against the worst hazards of nuclear proliferation must be legal and diplomatic. There must be further development of the kind of institutional arrangements provided in the Non-Proliferation Treaty. Countries will have to accept restrictions on their nuclear programs, such as submitting those programs to scrutiny in accordance with treaties and agreements and with contractual terms on which they import nuclear facilities, fuel, and technology. The motive will have to be a desire to participate in a more safeguarded nuclear world, with safeguards accepted on condition that other nations do likewise. Successful negotiation of such safeguards and restrictions will require, at the very least, effective federal control over the export of nuclear equipment, materials, and technology and vigorous efforts to work out terms and conditions of nuclear exports in common with the governments of other nuclear-exporting countries. Relaxation of safeguards must not be allowed to become a method of competition in the nuclear-export market.

The United States needs to cooperate with other governments to develop new methods of technical surveillance and intelligence to cope with a range of security and safety problems. As we have emphasized before, these problems include clandestine diversion of nuclear materials, theft of nuclear materials, hijacking of nuclear fuel shipments, sabotage of nuclear reactors or fuel facilities, and actions of any individual or organization attempting to make use of illicitly acquired nuclear materials. **The United States should support efforts to enlarge very substantially the inspection capability of the International Atomic Energy Agency, both through increased personnel and through the development and installation of the most modern techniques of automatic surveillance and materials control.**

It is time to join with other countries to plan for coping with possible nuclear emergencies. Governments could decide to abrogate the safeguards they have accepted under the treaty or under bilateral arrangements and proceed to build nuclear explosives. Nuclear accidents can occur; sabotage or occupation of nuclear facilities may be attempted; nonnational organizations or dissident military forces may acquire nuclear materials. Internal nuclear threats would have terrifying implications for other countries.

A world in which the ingredients for plutonium weapons are being shipped and stored and fabricated at a multitude of locations will be a world in which safeguards and security arrangements of a kind heretofore rare in this country may have to be imposed. The legal rights and obligations of interested governments may have to undergo redefinition. Planning for nuclear emergencies involves delicate issues of both national sovereignty and individual liberties. If skillfully done, this planning could help to develop and to reinforce a common interest in safeguarding against the more frightening contingencies.

Another problem that U.S. nuclear energy foreign policy must address is the disposal of nuclear wastes and the handling of other environmental hazards and problems. Little is certain about how the United States will manage the nuclear wastes produced within this country. In about ten years, hazardous nuclear wastes will be produced in scores of countries, some of which may lack suitable sites for temporary storage, many of which will have had little experience in handling such toxic materials. Waste disposal will be closely linked to safeguarding fuel supplies because the shipment of spent fuels to international storage facilities or to storage facilities within the fuel-producing countries would be determined by the location of those raw materials from which plutonium could be extracted. **We recommend that the United States participate in the collaborative development of techniques and facilities for handling inter-**

national shipments of nuclear materials and for disposing of radioactive waste materials in order to achieve common standards of physical security and safety.

INTERNATIONAL NUCLEAR FUEL FACILITIES

An important possibility in minimizing the dangers of plutonium reprocessing and uranium enrichment is the development of multinationally owned and operated nuclear fuel cycle facilities. Placing chemical-reprocessing facilities or uranium-enrichment facilities under the control of several nations might prevent individual nations from developing such facilities independently. The main purpose could be the renunciation by individual nations of national physical control over a potential nuclear weapons mobilization base on condition that other nations be bound by similar restraints. Such an arrangement would also make it possible to pool resources and take advantage of economies of scale, shared risks, and common methods of waste disposal. Another purpose might be to adopt unified security measures and safeguards for storage and transport of dangerous materials. These arrangements would by no means solve the security problems associated with the proliferation of nuclear energy, but they could help to reduce those dangers.

Development of multinational arrangements may require some initiative, some financing, and some inducements. An important possibility is that the United States could, together with other nations that produce reactors and reactor fuels for export, take some of that initiative and offer some of those inducements, possibly with the help of organizations such as the World Bank.

IAEA is examining a proposal for internationally owned and managed nuclear fuel centers. The U.S. government has expressed interest in this concept as a further way to reduce the incentives for developing indigenous fuel facilities with weapons potential. For example, on the condition that a significant number of countries in a given region will commit themselves to forgo independent national facilities, the United States should be prepared to consider contributing to the success of multilateral arrangements, possibly by making its own enrichment facilities available to participants in such an international program.*

To reduce the incentives for developing indigenous uranium-enrichment or plutonium-reprocessing facilities that might be usable for the production of weapons material, the United States should be prepared to

*See memorandum by LINCOLN GORDON, page 72.

offer, and to collaborate with other countries in offering, assured supplies of reactor fuel on long-term contracts at reasonable prices.* We are not prepared to offer a specific plan describing how all this might be done. The important point is that the United States, in cooperation with other nuclear-exporting nations, may be able to attach conditions to long-term contracts for nuclear fuel supply that would provide some of the inducement and initiative for arrangements of the kind we have outlined. In a world of competitive exports of both reactors and fuels, it is not likely that the United States alone could successfully attach conditions to the sale of reactor fuels that would be strong enough to induce such multinational developments. But many of the dangers of the plutonium economy and of the proliferation of uranium-enrichment facilities are going to be dangers to all countries participating in these nuclear developments. Skillful diplomacy may harness the self-interest of many countries.

Clearly, the United States cannot simultaneously take the initiative in promoting multinational fuel cycle facilities and unilaterally attempt to suppress the export of its technology. Unless other major potential exporters could be induced to participate, the United States could have only a modest short-term effect through a policy of export denial, and even that effort would appear offensively discriminatory unless it was coupled with alternative arrangements to assure fuel supplies and perhaps even to let the rest of the world participate in the planning and decision making where their crucial fuel supplies are concerned.

*See memorandum by CHARLES P. BOWEN, Jr., page 69.

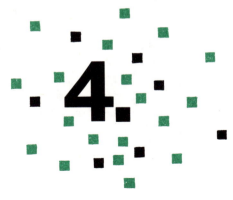

Formulating
an Energy Policy:
Our Greatest Need

ENERGY IS A NEW AND PREPONDERANT ELEMENT in both American foreign policy and world politics. It is also one of the most serious, most urgent, and longest-lasting problems for the American domestic economy. Hardly anything is more crucial to the present political and economic development of most countries than the cost of energy and the regularity of its supply over the long run. In the last few years, the central role of energy and natural resources in foreign policy and national security has become suddenly and dramatically evident. This is as true for the United States as it is for the rest of the world. Energy has been the greatest threat and the greatest challenge to American alliances, especially NATO. The changed nature of the world energy economy has had a stunning influence on international finance. The character of Middle Eastern strategy and politics reflects the recent developments in petroleum prices and the organization of the petroleum market.

Domestically, energy policy involves some crucial economic, environmental, and technological choices. Energy policy will impinge on public health and the quality of the environment. It will affect not only the cost of living but also the way energy costs are divided among different segments of the population. It is having a decisive impact on public fiscal and private financial policies and will continue to do so. Energy policy will have a major impact on where Americans live, how they travel, and what hazards they are exposed to.

The United States does not have two energy problems, one domestic and one foreign. They are the same problem. But that does not make it easier to solve. The U.S. government is accustomed to dealing with foreign problems and domestic problems separately. During the first quarter century after World War II, most domestic problems and policies had only a modest impact on U.S. foreign policy and on world politics. And during that period, foreign policy had a separate and manageable impact on the domestic economy.

Two separate energy problems calling for two separate energy policies might at least fit the federal government's framework and traditions. But a single pervasive problem, demanding a coherent set of policies that reflect the energy interdependence of the U.S. economy and the rest of the world, will require painful readjustments in the way the U.S. government makes policies and programs and carries them out.

This is a dramatic illustration of the U.S. government's need to develop quickly a new capability to deal coherently with matters that are of the highest diplomatic significance abroad and of the most urgent economic significance at home. There are foreign policy demands on the nuclear sector of the American economy that are wholly the responsibility of the federal government; there are domestic economic demands that will be a complex mixture of private enterprise and federal and state regulation and development.* *Acute national security interests and urgent economic and environmental interests at home are inextricably intertwined. They cannot be separated from similar interests of other countries. Failure of the U.S. government to recognize these interrelated interests and to deal with them in a coherent and comprehensive manner could be disastrous.*

There are currently a number of political initiatives to fragment energy policy by making it the responsibility of the individual states. To the extent that the object of these initiatives is obstruction, they represent a particularly futile and localized isolationism. To the extent that the object is to assure that energy policy is responsive to the local and regional needs of people, we believe that they are misguided. In the development of new sources of energy, in the provision of incentives to conserve energy, in balancing the energy needs of the nation against the social costs of exploiting resources, and especially in facing the problems of worldwide nuclear energy, this country cannot afford to have fifty separate energy policies. Security against the hazards of nuclear energy requires that the

*See memorandum by CHARLES P. BOWEN, Jr., page 72.

problems be faced on a scale larger than that of a single country, not fifty times smaller. Indeed, a unified national policy is inadequate if it is uncoordinated with the policies of the allied countries participating in IEA.

Nuclear energy, even more than oil and coal, will demand intergovernmental planning and undoubtedly new institutional arrangements. Nuclear energy will have to be handled in close coordination with petroleum and other forms of energy.

The United States cannot have a nuclear energy foreign policy unless it has an energy policy. It cannot have a foreign policy on reactor fuel supplies if it has no policy for domestic production of fuel. It cannot have a foreign policy on reprocessing spent fuel until it has settled domestic energy policy. The United States cannot take the lead in solving the problems of worldwide spent-fuel storage and waste disposal if it has no adequate plan for domestic storage and disposal or for participation in a larger plan. In general, this nation cannot assume any leadership or use whatever influence it might have in shaping the worldwide development of nuclear power except in coordination with domestic nuclear policies.

This does not mean formulating a separate domestic energy policy first and then turning to the rest of the world. It means that U.S. foreign policy in relation to energy cannot be any more effective and comprehensive than overall U.S. policy on energy, particularly nuclear energy.

Sensible energy planning in the United States must start by replacing the divisive ideological controversies about nuclear power with some basic understandings. We need a wider agreement that nuclear power does indeed raise severe problems, including hazards that are poorly understood and that may occur on an unprecedented scale. We need a candid recognition that however severe these problems are, they have to be acknowledged in order to be solved. We need a recognition that not all the problems can be solved to everybody's satisfaction in a hurry. Finally, we need a recognition that achieving high employment and improving the standard of living of all the American people will require meeting increasing demands for energy.*

Sensible energy planning also means recognizing that in planning the use of its coal resources for the decades to come, this country cannot afford to think exclusively of American needs. For example, the development of Japan and Japanese-American relations over the coming decade will be important to the security of the world, and Japan has little coal. Similarly, in planning the use of its uranium resources, this country cannot think exclusively of American needs. Decisions on federal funding for the

*See memorandum by LINCOLN GORDON, page 69.

development of a breeder reactor, decisions on the recycling of plutonium as a reactor fuel, federal programs of exploration to determine uranium reserves, and the financing of an increased capacity to provide nuclear reactor fuel must all be responsibly related to the energy needs and problems both of America's allies and of other countries. Otherwise, the United States risks maximizing its own standard of living while minimizing the security in which this standard of living can be enjoyed.

The development and conservation of energy resources will be central to the development of the U.S. economy during the coming decades. The increasing importance of energy policy was recognized by this Committee in *Achieving Energy Independence*, in which we recommended that energy policy should be the responsibility of a new cabinet-level agency. We reassert that recommendation. **We urge that any organizational arrangements for energy policy be undertaken with full recognition of the inseparability of the foreign and domestic aspects of national strategy for energy. From now on, energy policy must be considered an integral part of national security policy, and the highest level of presidential authority must be responsible for it.** There are a multitude of influences that will tend to make any cabinet-level agency that is concerned with energy more preoccupied with domestic issues than with foreign policy. But the final responsibility within the executive branch on major issues of energy policy *must* be settled at the highest level of presidential authority.*

GOVERNMENT ORGANIZATION FOR A SINGLE, COHERENT ENERGY POLICY

The Senate and the House of Representatives are not organized to deal effectively with the complex field of energy policy, particularly when this involves integrating long-term energy policies with foreign policy and national security. Like the executive branch, Congress has been traditionally accustomed to dealing with foreign problems and domestic problems separately. **We recommend that Congress take steps similar to those recommended by this Committee in 1974 for the executive branch to recognize that energy policy is simultaneously central to the domestic economy and to national security.**

Throughout the world, energy is going to be more subject to centralized planning and control than it was in the past. Environmental factors (both the quality of air and water and the beauty of the environment) are increasingly important in decisions about energy. Nuclear energy in-

*See memorandum by W. D. EBERLE, page 72.

volves unique security problems on both a national and an international scale. The private sector of the economy is not currently able to meet all the demands for planning and action. In the United States, the separate states' responsibilities for electric utility regulation and for environmental controls will need to be coordinated as this country moves into an era of large-scale development of nuclear energy.

One objective of U.S. nuclear energy policy will require a difficult choice among possible strategies. That objective is to inhibit the widespread development of independent fuel cycle facilities in individual countries. We need to discourage nations from developing their own facilities for enriching uranium or extracting plutonium from spent nuclear fuel. Unfortunately, the possible strategies for accomplishing this end compete with rather than reinforce each other. One choice would be to slow down U.S. research and development in uranium enrichment and abandon or indefinitely postpone the commercial reprocessing of spent fuel from American reactors. A second choice would be to refuse to license for export any reactors or any elements or components of the nuclear fuel cycle. A third choice would be to attempt, alone or through international arrangements, to guarantee the supply of reactor fuel at reasonable cost, thereby making heavy investment in independent national facilities for the production of reactor fuel economically unnecessary and perhaps unattractive. Still another choice would be the effort to conduct fuel cycle processes on an international or multinational basis so that most of the facilities and inventories would be subject to the restraining ownership and control of several governments and constrained by treaties or other commitments. This problem is an example of the important decisions that involve major implications for U.S. foreign policy and that the U.S. government must soon make.

Another such decision concerns the development of additional capacity to produce nuclear fuel for power reactors and U.S. export policy regarding nuclear fuel. Decisions on the reprocessing of spent fuel for the extraction of plutonium and on the use of plutonium as a nuclear fuel are even more crucial. Should the United States proceed with, accelerate, or slow down development of the breeder reactor and other advanced reactor technologies? How can the exploration and mining of uranium ore be speeded up both here and abroad? What is the U.S. government's proper role in the ownership, control, or management of supplies, stockpiles, and prices of nuclear fuels? What arrangement can the United States make to assure governments that there will not be shortages of fuel for vital and expensive electric power reactors in which they will be investing in the coming years? Should important parts of the nuclear fuel cycle be developed through international rather than national ownership and control? What international arrangements for coping with physical safeguards on fissionable materials can be devised between the signers and the non-signers of the Non-Proliferation Treaty?

The political metaphor of "one world" is gradually becoming a reality. For two decades, it has been technically possible (through intercontinental aircraft or intercontinental ballistic missiles) for the United States and the Soviet Union to threaten whole metropolitan areas with sudden destruction. The time is coming when any fishing boat may carry undetected a bomb that could devastate several square miles using a by-product of a worldwide electric power industry. However unpromising it may be to strive for that world's safety through a vigorous foreign policy, there can be no hope whatever in a policy that treats nuclear energy strictly as a domestic issue to be handled outside the framework of foreign policy and defense.

No matter how successfully governments manage safeguards, one strategic fact will remain: With the continuing development of nuclear electric power, more governments will possess the independent ability to produce nuclear weapons. Multilateral diplomacy can hope to keep governments from openly acquiring nuclear weapons. The most that even multilateral diplomacy can hope to achieve would be to induce governments to accept and to comply with safeguards against the secret assembly of weapons. Wars and military emergencies are conditions under which governments that *have* nuclear weapons might consider *using* nuclear weapons. In twenty years, most of the world's governments will *have* (and will be *known* to have) a capacity to mobilize nuclear materials and technology into nuclear weapons. The most fundamental problem of international security will then be to prevent any interest in using nuclear weapons from ever being realized.

Memoranda of Comment, Reservation, or Dissent

Page 11, by CHARLES P. BOWEN, JR.

The core issue is not given adequate exposure, and the related pertinent questions are not posed. Given all the negotiations, inspections, agreements, economic inducements, diplomatic or other pressures, and treaties, what is to be done about the open or surreptitious violator? How and how quickly? By what institutions?

Although it was clearly not within the paper's scope to offer solutions to these vital questions, the statement falls far short of sufficiently emphasizing their awesome nature and overriding importance. It is imperative that the major powers individually and collectively develop and announce specific policies and practices to cope with violators. However unpleasant or impolitic the answers and resulting practices may be, reliance upon pious hopes that no need for applying them will arise is a tragic kind of wishful thinking. The frequently demonstrated incapacity of the world community to deal with even small groups of terrorists underlines the pertinence of this view. Arguments that these represent special political situations are without merit. There will be such situations for the foreseeable future.

Page 11, by LINCOLN GORDON

I would have preferred to defer this statement until CED was in a position to make considered recommendations on several of the critical issues brought out in the text. I vigorously support the basic points that American nuclear energy policy cannot be made unilaterally, in disregard of nuclear developments in the rest of the world; that our example will not be automatically followed elsewhere; that our leverage and influence are limited, although by no means negligible; and that our security will be better served by an active international energy policy than by ostrichlike energy chauvinism. If the genie of large-scale atomic power from nuclear fission is irrevocably out of the bottle, then we should focus on international action to minimize the incentives to weapons proliferation and the hazards created by such proliferation.

In this text, however, we step up to a number of critical issues without pointing to conclusions. Cardinal examples are the chemical reprocessing of spent fuels (which should be deferred pending intensive international negotiations to strengthen safeguards), the decision between public and private responsibility for the immediate requirements of increased uranium enrichment, desirable limitations on export of fuel and facilities pending negotiation of stronger safeguards among the entire group of exporting countries, and inclusion of U.S. facilities in regional arrangements for multinational control of enrichment or reprocessing plants. Other closely related issues are unmentioned, for example, the possibility of regional nuclear centers designed to minimize shipments of enriched, reprocessed, or spent fuels.

In short, having gone this far, I believe that CED should have taken the requisite time and effort to find its best answers to the vital questions the statement poses.

Page 11, by PHILIP SPORN

With some exceptions, I can accept the recommendations of this report.

Yet, a reading of the summary finds me perplexed and bewildered. The cause of my dismay is the treatment of the problem as if it were nothing more than a highly complicated technological, legal, and diplomatic affair that, by much dedicated study, can somehow be resolved by developing a new worldwide treaty or organization. It seems to me that this does not sufficiently consider the consequences of the failure of such an organization that we would have to face. The stark fact is that the proliferation of atomic bomb material raises perhaps the most threatening issue that has confronted man and his place on planet Earth since the advent of the three great monotheisms. Each of these for the first time offered its own answer to man's perplexing question: What and why am I? Now, with man's very ability to survive at stake, this question has become heavily complicated, so that it has become more atavistic: How can I be?

Surely, with so much trembling in the balance, we cannot permit ourselves to be overawed by technics, formulas, legalities, and diplomatic arrangements and leave assurance of man's survival on planet Earth entirely up to the governments of the world to provide. Governments today, as was true of governments 1,000 and 5,000 years ago, can be craven, vacillating, immoral.

In my footnote to page 20, I suggested study of the possibilities of developing anti-nuclear-terror terrorist organizations. But for the long range, if we are successful to assure the life of man on planet Earth, we need to appeal to and summon power and forces over and above government. We need to bring about a powerful revolution in man's dominant, religious dedication to the life force and to join universally in a great moral life-saving movement to prevent the disappearance of life on Earth. This is going to be a difficult and long task. We must, therefore, start at once. I have been encouraged in that belief by the recent refreshing observation of Governor Brown, a political novice but a man of unique strength of character and deep moral convictions, that what the nation most needs in the making of foreign policy is a moral base. Who is better set up to give the world this leadership than the United States, and why should not CED sound this clear, hope-giving note in this report?

Page 14, by PHILIP SPORN

Witness the recent dispatch from Paris that appeared in *Science*, July 23, 1976:

> Despite the emergence of an antinuclear opposition in France, marked notably by a protest by 400 scientists last year, and the dire warnings voiced in the so-called nuclear debate in the United States, the French government shows little sign of having serious second thoughts about their nuclear decision.

Page 20, by PHILIP SPORN

I am frankly dismayed at the trust placed in "more complicated legal and diplomatic safeguards" and in "wisdom and subtlety" in the formulation of U.S. security policy suggested in the preceding paragraph. Just how reliable are more complicated legal and diplomatic safeguards going to be in a showdown, and with all the wisdom and subtlety, will they prove to be more effective than mere scraps of paper?

Page 20, by PHILIP SPORN

I am even more dismayed at the categorical dismissal of the idea of channeling "funds into military forces in the hope that money can always buy something useful." The report clearly developed "the possibility of theft or hijacking for criminal or terrorist purposes." If that is so, why not study the possibilities of organizing to thwart terrorist purposes? Was the rescue raid that saved the lives of more than 100 innocent people that the Israeli commandos brought off on July 3 at Entebbe Airport a military operation, or was it effected by the "more complicated legal and diplomatic safeguards"? And with the recent rejection by the Security Council of a condemnation of terrorism (with our ally in detente joining in that refusal), why not channel some funds into bold, but not necessarily bankruptingly expensive, organizations that will strike terror into the hearts of terrorists bent upon active nuclear terror?

Pages 21 and 62, by LINCOLN GORDON

I agree with the implication that a policy of zero energy growth is not compatible with high employment and a better standard of living. On the other hand, there are sufficient opportunities for conservation so that the energy growth rate could be greatly reduced for a number of years. That issue, however, is not central to the problem of nuclear energy because even with zero energy growth, it would be necessary to replace oil and gas progressively by other energy sources as the petroleum era approaches its end.

Page 24, by LINCOLN GORDON

I endorse this suggestion and believe that it should have been included among the boldface recommendations in this summary.

Pages 24 and 59, by CHARLES P. BOWEN, JR.

As made clear in earlier paragraphs, economics is not likely to be the controlling factor in countries with irrational international political objectives.

Pages 25 and 52, by LINCOLN GORDON

The logic of the facts and of the discussion clearly favors governmental responsibility for the interim phase of expanded enrichment by gaseous diffusion. We should have so recommended.

Pages 25 and 52, by LINCOLN GORDON

The logic of the statement as a whole points strongly toward postponement of the decision on reprocessing pending a strenuous effort to negotiate stronger international safeguards. We should have so recommended.

Page 26, by JAMES T. HILL, JR.

I fully concur in the recommendation that we "unhobble" our position as a nuclear supplier as a necessary means for inducing other nations to abstain from developing fuel facilities that have weapons potential. I would only observe that although this course of action represents our best hope for inhibiting the development by other nations of fuel facilities that have dangerous weapons potentials, the problem outlined in note 5 on page 44 cannot be ignored. Dependence on the United States for nuclear fuels may prove to be suspect and unappealing to other nations, just as dependence on the United States for coal (assuming this were a truly viable alternative to OPEC oil over the long term—a questionable assumption at best) might well be suspect and unappealing, as suggested. This is a matter with which we shall have to deal sensitively and imaginatively. It should not be regarded as an insuperable hurdle.

Page 27, by PHILIP SPORN

I would like to restate the last sentence as follows: "The most fundamental purpose of national security will be to prevent a capacity to mobilize nuclear materials developing into an interest in using these as nuclear weapons."

Page 40, by LINCOLN GORDON

This statement correctly opposes a general embargo on exports of nuclear materials, equipment, and technology, but it goes too far in opposing any restraint whatever on such exports. The case for restraint on exports to India is very strong. Considering the length of time that will be required to implement the kind of negotiations "strongly recommended" on pages 22 and 56, a judicious interim policy of strengthening conditions on exports certainly seems called for.

Page 43, by LINCOLN GORDON

In reflecting on how far the case of August 1945 might be a precedent, it is also relevant to recall that, at that time, there was no possibility of retaliation of any kind, nuclear or nonnuclear, from any source. Such a condition will never again exist.

Pages 44, 45, and 47, by JAMES T. HILL, JR.

In our proper concern to create awareness of the perils of the imminent emergence of a new form of nuclear proliferation, we must avoid at all costs any minimization of the continuing perils that Soviet nuclear capability and expansionism pose. It would be folly of the worst sort to shift our emphasis or concentration onto coping with the newly emerging terror of a different species of nuclear proliferation at the expense of maintaining a nuclear capability fully adequate to discourage or deter Soviet expansionism or adventurism. The Soviet threat is present and palpable and certain; it is not distant or problematical. There is hope in the fact that the Soviets must or should view the threat of the approaching nuclear proliferation with genuine concern. The dangers of an increasingly unstable nuclear world, with all the potential destruction, potential acts of irrational terrorism, and potential for spontaneous combustion, may provide a basis for new forms of U.S.-Soviet cooperation and multination action that, while containing or at least reducing the threats of the new nuclear dangers, will contribute to deterring or at least lessening the very real terrors of U.S.-Soviet nuclear confrontation. This presents both a new challenge and a new opportunity to U.S. diplomatic initiative and ingenuity. It is complicated by the fact that the Soviet Union and the Warsaw Pact nations enjoy a superiority in conventional, nonnuclear forces that is offset or neutralized by U.S. and NATO capabilities in the nuclear area (including tactical nuclear weapons). Until there can be a stabilization in the area of conventional forces and weapons in comparison with the Soviets, any neutralization of our nuclear strength, whether through a no-first-use declaration or otherwise, would tip the balance in favor of the Soviets, would invite Soviet adventurism and expansionism, and would foster new elements of instability in East-West relations.

To reiterate, the arrival on the world scene of a potentially terrible new nuclear threat cannot be permitted to become the occasion for the neglect of a very real, very menacing existing threat. To divert our attention from the Soviet threat, to lag in the maintenance of our nuclear deterrent with regard to the Soviets would be to court disaster. The only prescription is to commence immediately in the ways indicated in this statement to accept, face up to, and find answers for the new nuclear dangers while steadfastly exerting the necessary efforts to deal effectively with the existing nuclear dangers.

Page 58, by LINCOLN GORDON

This is an important recommendation that should have appeared in boldface in the summary of recommendations in Chapter 1.

Page 61, by CHARLES P. BOWEN, JR.

Mention of state interest in nuclear regulation, even in parentheses, is inconsistent with the earlier decrying of fifty different policies.

Page 63, by W. D. EBERLE

It is fine to exhort the U.S. executive and Congress to be better organized, but to recommend that this be done as part of achieving an energy policy will postpone results on both. What is needed is a commitment to a cabinet-level appointee who shall formulate, coordinate, and recommend energy policy with presidential and congressional backing. This could better be accomplished as it was in international trade, with the Office of the Special Representative for Trade, who is responsible to several congressional committees as well as to the President and has the power to coordinate interagency executive branch policy and to work directly with Congress. A limited life of five years on such an office would be useful.

The new energy office should be created through a congressional act and then implemented by a presidential executive order so that you have both congressional support and the clear set of intercabinet powers. Creating this office is politically possible because its creation does not create a new cabinet member or a reshuffling of responsibilities for cabinet members or of congressional committees wherein either group can stall or veto such reorganization. Such single-area focus on problem solving on a day-to-day basis should bring support. This solution is quite different from the noncoordinated cabinet-level responsibility, such as the Resources Council, FEA, and ERDA, none of which have the overall backing or responsibility. Its responsibilities should include not only atomic energy but also, as stated in the 1974 CED policy statement *Achieving Energy Independence,* all other forms of energy so that coordinated policy recommendations can be made.

Energy solutions are needed now by better-coordinated substantive policy recommendations from both the executive and Congress. This must be the priority, not to achieve a basic government reorganization, even though that may be desirable.

APPENDIX A

OPERATING TIME AND PLUTONIUM QUALITY

THE TECHNICAL CONSIDERATIONS that determine the length of time the fuel operates in a reactor are of some significance to this study. The uranium fuel elements in a power reactor are typically allowed to operate for about three years in the reactor before removal. Removal and replenishment is on a staggered schedule, a third of the fuel being replaced each year; and the reactor has to be closed down for this operation, which takes about a month. Both the frequency of renewal and the total time before removal represent a balance among several cost considerations. The fuel could operate longer if left in the reactor for more than three years, but its efficiency would be impaired; and if the fuel assemblies were much less expensive, the spent fuel might be extracted after a shorter time because of the superior operating and handling characteristics of the fresher fuel.

One characteristic of the spent fuel is that it contains not only the fissionable plutonium 239 (the plutonium that can be both a fuel and an explosive) but other plutonium isotopes as well. These other isotopes are not separated from the plutonium 239 in the chemical processing that separates plutonium from the rest of the waste products. And they impair the quality of the plutonium as an explosive. Furthermore, the proportion in which the undesirable isotopes are produced in the reactor increases with the time that the uranium fuel is left in the reactor. For purposes of making explosives, earlier extraction of the spent fuel would result in a less contaminated supply of plutonium 239.

Thus, the most economic use of uranium fuel for the production of electric power is not the same as the optimal use of a reactor in the production of weapons-grade plutonium. And the plutonium that would be shipped and inventoried for use as reactor fuel would not be the highest-grade plutonium for making explosives. It could be fabricated into bombs, but bombs made of that plutonium would have reduced explosive power, require larger amounts of material, and perhaps be less reliable. (Nevertheless, a bomb with only 1 to 5 percent of the energy yield of the plutonium bomb that destroyed Nagasaki could be compacted in a container that could be carried in a passenger automobile and would be equivalent to several hundred tons of TNT.)

A government that had seriously determined to embark on a plutonium weapons program would therefore consider removing spent fuel from a power reactor after a much shorter period than the usual three-year burning life. Removal of such comparatively fresh fuel assemblies would of course be evident under the inspection arrangements to which the signatories of the Non-Proliferation Treaty have committed themselves, and a government could be challenged to explain the action.

APPENDIX B

WORLD NUCLEAR POWER PLANTS IN OPERATION, UNDER CONSTRUCTION, OR ON ORDER AS OF DECEMBER 31, 1975[a]

Country	Number of Nuclear Power Reactors in Operation	Current Total Nuclear Generating Capacity (MWe)[b]	Number of Nuclear Power Reactors under Construction or on Order	Total Nuclear Generating Capacity under Construction or on Order (MWe)	Party to Non-Proliferation Treaty
ARGENTINA	1	319	1	600	No
AUSTRIA	—	—	1	692	Yes
BELGIUM	3	1,650	4	3,797	Yes
BRAZIL	—	—	3	2,626	No
BULGARIA	2	880	2	880	Yes
CANADA	6	2,512	14	9,324	Yes

(continued)

Country	Number of Nuclear Power Reactors in Operation	Current Total Nuclear Generating Capacity (MWe)[b]	Number of Nuclear Power Reactors under Construction or on Order	Total Nuclear Generating Capacity under Construction or on Order (MWe)	Party to Non-Proliferation Treaty
CZECHOSLOVAKIA	1	110	4	1,760	Yes
FINLAND	—	—	4	2,160	Yes
FRANCE	10	2,818	20	18,478	No
GERMANY (DEMOCRATIC REPUBLIC)	3	950	4	1,760	Yes
GERMANY (FEDERAL REPUBLIC)	9	4,869	17	18,393	Yes
HUNGARY	—	—	4	1,760	Yes
INDIA	3	602	5	1,082	No
IRAN	—	—	4	4,200	Yes
ITALY	4	1,387	5	3,908	Yes
JAPAN	12	6,396	12	9,109	Yes
KOREA (SOUTH)	—	—	3	1,798	Yes

(continued)

Country	Number of Nuclear Power Reactors in Operation	Current Total Nuclear Generating Capacity (MWe)[b]	Number of Nuclear Power Reactors under Construction or on Order	Total Nuclear Generating Capacity under Construction or on Order (MWe)	Party to Non-Proliferation Treaty
LUXEMBOURG	—	—	1	1,300	Yes
MEXICO	—	—	2	1,320	Yes
NETHERLANDS	2	532	—	—	Yes
PAKISTAN	1	125	—	—	No
PHILIPPINES	—	—	2	1,252	Yes
POLAND	—	—	1	440	Yes
ROMANIA	—	—	1	440	Yes
SOVIET UNION	10	3,285	15	11,080	Yes
SPAIN	3	1,073	8	7,242	No
SWEDEN	5	3,169	6	5,180	Yes
SWITZERLAND	3	1,006	5	4,847	No

(continued)

(continued)

Country	Number of Nuclear Power Reactors in Operation	Current Total Nuclear Generating Capacity (MWe)[b]	Number of Nuclear Power Reactors under Construction or on Order	Total Nuclear Generating Capacity under Construction or on Order (MWe)	Party to Non-Proliferation Treaty
TAIWAN	—	—	6	4,924	Yes
UNITED KINGDOM	31	6,810	8	4,950	Yes
UNITED STATES	64	46,337	150	163,998	Yes
YUGOSLAVIA	—	—	1	615	Yes

[a]The following countries had no known nuclear power installations in operation, under construction, or on order as of December 31, 1975, but had at least one nuclear reactor or element of the nuclear fuel cycle in their territory: Australia, Central African Republic, Chile, Colombia, Denmark, Egypt, Gabon, Greece, Indonesia, Iraq, Israel, Niger, Norway, People's Republic of China, Portugal, South Africa, Thailand, Turkey, Uruguay, Venezuela, Vietnam, Zaire.

[b]Megawatts of electricity.

SOURCE: *Nuclear News Buyers Guide,* February 1976.

Objectives of the Committee for Economic Development

For three decades, the Committee for Economic Development has had a respected influence on business and public policy. Composed of two hundred leading business executives and educators, CED is devoted to these two objectives:

To develop, through objective research and informed discussion, findings and recommendations for private and public policy which will contribute to preserving and strengthening our free society, achieving steady economic growth at high employment and reasonably stable prices, increasing productivity and living standards, providing greater and more equal opportunity for every citizen, and improving the quality of life for all.

To bring about increasing understanding by present and future leaders in business, government, and education and among concerned citizens of the importance of these objectives and the ways in which they can be achieved.

CED's work is supported strictly by private voluntary contributions from business and industry, foundations, and individuals. It is independent, nonprofit, nonpartisan, and nonpolitical.

The two hundred trustees, who generally are presidents or board chairmen of corporations and presidents of universities, are chosen for their individual capacities rather than as representatives of any particular interests. By working with scholars, they unite business judgment and experience with scholarship in analyzing the issues and developing recommendations to resolve the economic problems that constantly arise in a dynamic and democratic society.

Through this business-academic partnership, CED endeavors to develop policy statements and other research materials that commend themselves as guides to public and business policy; for use as texts in college economics and political science courses and in management training courses; for consideration and discussion by newspaper and magazine editors, columnists, and commentators; and for distribution abroad to promote better understanding of the American economic system.

CED believes that by enabling businessmen to demonstrate constructively their concern for the general welfare, it is helping business to earn and maintain the national and community respect essential to the successful functioning of the free enterprise capitalist system.

Statements on National Policy Issued by the Research and Policy Committee *(publications in print)*

*Statements issued in association with CED counterpart organizations in foreign countries.

Improving Federal Program Performance *(September 1971)*

Social Responsibilities of Business Corporations *(June 1971)*

Education for the Urban Disadvantaged:
  From Preschool to Employment *(March 1971)*

Further Weapons Against Inflation *(November 1970)*

Making Congress More Effective *(September 1970)*

*Development Assistance to Southeast Asia *(July 1970)*

Training and Jobs for the Urban Poor *(July 1970)*

Improving the Public Welfare System *(April 1970)*

Reshaping Government in Metropolitan Areas *(February 1970)*

Economic Growth in the United States *(October 1969)*

Assisting Development in Low-Income Countries *(September 1969)*

*Nontariff Distortions of Trade *(September 1969)*

Fiscal and Monetary Policies for Steady Economic Growth *(January 1969)*

Financing a Better Election System *(December 1968)*

Innovation in Education: New Directions for the American School *(July 1968)*

Modernizing State Government *(July 1967)*

*Trade Policy Toward Low-Income Countries *(June 1967)*

How Low Income Countries Can Advance Their Own Growth *(September 1966)*

Modernizing Local Government *(July 1966)*

A Better Balance in Federal Taxes on Business *(April 1966)*

Budgeting for National Objectives *(January 1966)*

Educating Tomorrow's Managers *(October 1964)*

Improving Executive Management in the Federal Government *(July 1964)*

Trade Negotiations for a Better Free World Economy *(May 1964)*

Economic Literacy for Americans *(March 1962)*

Statements issued in association with CED counterpart organizations in foreign countries.